ROMANCING THE HOME

ROMANCING THE HOME

*How to Have a
Marriage That Sizzles*

ED YOUNG

BROADMAN & HOLMAN PUBLISHERS
Nashville, Tennessee

© Copyright 1994
BROADMAN & HOLMAN PUBLISHERS
All rights reserved

4261-59
ISBN: 0-8054-6159-0

Dewey Decimal Classification: 306.81
Subject Heading: HOME // MARRIAGE
Library of Congress Card Catalog Number: 93-4579
Printed in the United States of America

Unless otherwise stated, all Scripture quotations are from the Holy Bible, *New American Standard Bible,* copyright © The Lockman Foundation, 1960, 1962, 1963, 1968, 1971, 1972, 1973, 1975, 1977. Used by permission.

Library of Congress Cataloging-in-Publication Data

Young, Ed
    Romancing the home: how to have a marriage that sizzles / Ed Young
p. cm.
    ISBN 0-8054-6159-0
    1. Marriage—United States.   2. Marriage—Religious aspects—Christianity.
        I. Young, Ed   II. Title.
HQ734.Y814   1994
646.7'8—dc20   93-4579
                                                       CIP

WHEN I THINK OF SIZZLE IN A MAR-
riage, I think of my wife of 34 years, JoBeth. She is
definitely responsible for keeping romance alive and
exciting in our home. I am reminded of the husband
who joked that he was the "model" husband—a
"model" being defined as an imitation of the real thing.
As a wife, and in all her other roles as well, JoBeth is
definitely "the real thing." The depth of our love and
the relationship we share is primarily the result of both
God's grace and the countless ways JoBeth graciously
surpasses the biblical standards of Proverbs 31 every
single day of our life together. This book is lovingly
dedicated to the "sizzle" of my life: my beloved Joby.

Acknowledgments

First, let me express special gratitude to Leigh McLeroy. She has translated the spoken word into written form. Additionally, she has expanded and embellished those spoken words so that they have more sense and significance on the printed page than the original "pulpit edition" had. This was certainly no easy task, in light of my extemporaneous approach to communication. Leigh is a dedicated and exceedingly gifted writer whose biblical perspective on marriage has greatly enhanced the value of this book.

My office staff supports me daily in a host of ways. Beverly Gambrell, my research assistant, supplies a steady stream of up-to-date information on numerous topics, and helps me express fundamental truths in contemporary language. My administrative assistant, Linda Richard, has protected, helped and encouraged me for many years. She is my right hand—she keeps me on track. The kind voice of Gay Dees is the first many hear when they reach my office. Her loyalty and grace under pressure are valuable gifts. I am grateful to these and many others whose unique contributions allow me to more effectively serve in the work to which God has called me.

CONTENTS

INTRODUCTION

ONE LEADING PSYCHOTHERAPIST, after nearly 30 years of studying men, women, and the human condition, said, "I ask myself, *what is it women want?*" That question still mystifies most men. And many women could honestly ask the same question about the men in their lives. Yet we still desire one another, and long for permanent, intimate relationships in marriage. In fact, a recent poll of American adults by the *Los Angeles Times* reports that an overwhelming number of persons, when asked what their main goal in life was, responded "to be happily married." Why, then, do nearly half the marriages begun in the United States eventually end in divorce? And why do many of the marriages that technically survive have so little life and health?

I believe part of the reason is that we do not understand and put into practice God's principles. He invented marriage, He ordained the institution, and He knows best how it is to function. We have paid too little attention to His precepts in this most intimate area of human life. Second, we have failed to understand one another. Cecil Osborne said years ago that "the difficulty of achieving a happy marriage is compounded by the fact that men and women are basically incompat-

1

ible, in that they have goals, needs, emotions, and drives which are incompatible with those of the opposite sex."[1]

Dr. Willard Harley, a psychotherapist and marriage and family therapist, expounded on this idea more recently in an insightful book entitled *His Needs Her Needs*. In it he related five basic needs of men and five basic needs of women in marriage, based on his observation of countless couples in therapy. As Osborne suggested previously, they were completely different. In *Romancing the Home*, we look first at God's design for marriage, then at several of these conflicting needs of husbands and wives, with an eye toward building a marriage that does not just survive but really sizzles.

This book began as a series of messages called "A Marriage That Sizzles" for the Second Baptist Church family in Houston, Texas. They were later aired on "The Winning Walk," a half-hour program of Bible teaching, music, and testimony that is broadcast nationally and internationally. The flood of mail received as a result indicates that there are thousands of men and women who are not experiencing the adventure and romance of marriage as God designed it.

Even in a culture that has low expectations and diminished regard for the institution of marriage, we are bombarded with books on the subject. Many of them are before-the-fact "how-to's" or after-the-fact "what-now's." Certainly there is a need for marriage preparation and divorce recovery books. But I believe the real need is in giving help and hope to those who are in the midst of marriage and wondering, *Is this all there is?*

Every man and woman comes to marriage with a host of needs and unmet desires. Whether their union will prove to be a rich, lifetime adventure or a lackluster life-sentence depends on their willingness to follow God's design, and their determination to consider one another's needs as more important than their own. Husbands and wives committed to understanding God's plan and their own differing needs make a solid beginning at "romancing the home."

I do not believe there is a marriage in existence today that would not benefit from both partners asking themselves: *What is it like being married to me?* Honest answers to this question could set a real-life romance in motion that would fulfill its partners, inspire countless others, and glorify the God who gave man and woman to one another in the beginning. And the home is the perfect setting for such a romance. "The most dramatic things," said G. K. Chesterton, "happen at home, from being born to being dead. What a man thinks about these things is his life: and to substitute for them a bustle of electioneering and legislation is to wander among screens and pulleys on the wrong side of pasteboard scenery; and never to act the play. And that play is always a miracle play; and the name of the hero is Everyman."[2]

May your home and mine be alive with the kind of real romance that is born in the light of God's love and grows in the application of His truth.

PART ONE

HO-HUM HUSBANDS AND WORN-OUT WIVES

1

IN NAME
ONLY

IT BEGAN WELL. THE STUFF OF FAIRY
tales always does. A worldly wise, 30-something bachelor chose a shy young schoolteacher to be his bride. If
he seemed less than lovestruck, the world was quickly
smitten. Their storybook wedding was performed by
the Archbishop of Canterbury, attended by world leaders and heads of state, and watched by millions of
ordinary people. After a long and luxurious honeymoon cruise and a few idyllic days in Scotland secluded
from worldly intrusion, real married life began.

Twelve years later, the marriage ended, not in divorce, but rather in a formal division. They would
remain husband and wife, but in name only. She would
be allowed certain freedoms in exchange for "keeping
up appearances." He would maintain a separate residence and a separate identity. Royalty has its privileges,

no doubt, but the marriage of the Prince and Princess of Wales, which began with such pomp and promise, looks today remarkably like hundreds and thousands of other, less privileged domestic unions.

Explanations abound, of course, after the fact. She was too young; he was too preoccupied. Other parties were involved; old romantic alliances were not dissolved; family intrusions were insurmountable; the scrutiny of the press was crippling. Their differences, exciting at first, became irritating in time. Their roles became reversed as he wryly noted, "I seem to do nothing but collect flowers these days." She became more independent than either of them imagined she might: "When we were first married, I needed Charles by my side. Now I can cope on my own." Then finally, "I'll go out and do my bit in the way I know how, and I'll leave him behind."[1] Statements issued by Buckingham Palace confirmed what Charles and Diana had already telegraphed by innuendo to friends, acquaintances, reporters, and subjects: the legal union might well survive, but the marriage had died.

The home is the perfect setting for romance, and no matter how long you've been married, you can have a marriage that sizzles!

Statistically speaking, half the marriages in America do not survive "till death do us part." Realistically speaking, many of those that do simply exist in name only. We seem to be living in a land of ho-hum husbands and worn-out wives, all going through the motions of marriage, but missing the magic of committed love. The very thought of romance in the home seems foreign—and the idea that marriage can "sizzle" is obviously reserved for the very newly-wed. But I believe that the home is the perfect setting for romance, and that no matter how long you've been married—or to whom you're married!—you can have a marriage that sizzles!

Marriage has a bad reputation today. It is entered into lightly or avoided at all costs; it is routinely demeaned by celebrities, social commentators, and the mass media. But marriage itself is not the problem. The concept of one man together in a covenant with one woman for life is still sound. Despite all the marriages that fail, we are still marrying one another with great hope and expectation. A recent *L.A. Times* poll of 2,000 adults revealed that the overwhelming majority, when asked about their main goal in life, responded "to be happily married." What, then, has gone wrong?

Do You Believe in Magic?

Some people have a magical view of marriage. They harbour the idea that one day they will be "zapped" into the presence of someone of the opposite sex who is so compelling, so "right," that they will know without a doubt this is the one they are to marry. The feeling of falling in love will overwhelm all doubt, all logic, all reason. Some writers have even called this phenomenon "touching the magic."

Do you believe in magic? Do you see love as a mystical power that is totally irresistible and impossible to control? If you do, and you marry on that basis, the odds are high that your marriage will at worst end in tragedy and disaster, and at best be a tremendous disappointment. Beginning a marriage on the basis of feelings alone is simply not enough.

I seldom meet someone who does not know my vocation, but recently my wife JoBeth and I met a 32-year-old woman who knew nothing about me. She was single, and in a short while, the conversation turned to the topic of marriage. I was so excited by the possibility of getting a real, "un-churchified" response on the subject that I pressed on enthusiastically.

"Do you ever hope to fall in love?" I asked.

"Oh, yes," she replied.

"How do you think it will happen?"

"I don't know," she said. "I guess I'll just meet someone, and, you know, boom."

I took a different tack. "What are some of the characteristics you'd like to find in this person who will be your mate?"

"Well," she said, "I want someone who loves me."

"That's good," I said. "That's a good beginning."

She then began to pick up steam. "I want somebody who will work . . . at least who will pay their own way. And I want someone who will take me out once in a while. I don't want to stay at home all the time. Not every night—but I'd like to go out."

"Nothing wrong with that," I concurred.

She kept going. "I want someone who loves kids and wants to have a family. That's important. And someone who likes dogs. I just love dogs—I have two. Yeah, they'd have to love animals."

"That makes sense," I said. "Can you think of anything else?"

She thought for a while. "No, I really can't think of anything that wouldn't fall into one of those categories. That's it. That's all."

"Let me suggest something to you," I said after she had described the perfect man in as much detail as she could muster, "something that you've left off your list that you might want to add."

She was curious, I could tell. There is no better audience to preach to than one who doesn't know you're a preacher.

"If you added this one thing to your list, I believe all the other characteristics you've mentioned would be there, plus a whole lot more," I suggested.

"What would that be?" she asked.

"Let me just press a minute, and suggest that if you found a guy who believed there was a God and knew that God, then that fellow could meet all your requirements, and more."

She repeated my words, "Believed there was a God and really knew that God?"

"That's right," I said.

She thought for a long time, and finally she responded. "Yeah. That would be great. That would be super. I'll put that on my list."

"I don't mean to be troublesome," I said, "but I think we've got a problem. If you find a guy who believes there is a God and knows that God, he's going to be looking for a girl who knows Him too." And in a few moments, I had a chance to share with her, and to seek to point her to Jesus Christ.

> *When feeling becomes the dominant force in a relationship, the relationship is bound for trouble because feelings change.*

The moral of the story is this: Far too many of us have the idea that lasting love is based on emotion and feeling, period. While I would be the last person to dismiss the importance of emotion and feeling and passion in love, I believe that when feeling becomes the dominant force in a relationship, the relationship is bound for trouble. Why? Because feelings change.

THOUGHTS OF THE HEART

My favorite definition of feelings is a purely poetic one: feelings are thoughts of the heart, instead of thoughts of the mind. The trouble is that hearts can change just as easily as minds can change. I'm reminded of the fellow who said, "I have a feeling or the feeling has me, until another feeling takes the place of the feeling I felt. Once I had this feeling, and I felt like it had always been there, but when that feeling left, I felt like it had never been around. When that feeling returned, I felt like it had never departed." Kind of makes your head spin, doesn't it?

If you are letting feelings control you, your marriage and your decision-making—you are in for a tough road. And if your life is run on the basis of feelings, you are living the life of a child. But many people do exactly that. I think there are several reasonable explanations why this happens.

First, children are exposed to popular culture through stories—wonderful stories about Prince Charming riding in on a white horse to rescue a beautiful young princess. He would kiss her—after they fell in love at first sight—and the two would live happily ever after. No mention was made of his employment status, her family, subsequent children, or ex-girlfriends or boyfriends. That would be too un-romantic. In fairy tale after fairy tale they met, fell in love, married, and lived trouble-free forever. And so, many children began by thinking that is what marriage is all about.

Then they get a little older and television, movies, and romance novels reinforce these romantic illusions. Boy meets girl, and love runs its course, overcoming every obstacle. True love seems to conquer all, and in the time it takes to sing a song or view a sitcom!

By the time most people approach marriage, they are so weighted down by cultural baggage and bad examples that they are ill-equipped to forge a lifetime union.

Second, even though children's own families do not live up to this fantasy, they cling to the illusion that a perfect, troublefree marriage is possible.

One in three children will grow up in a home where one parent is absent due to divorce. Imagine the longing for romance and rescue intensified in the crucible of a broken home. By the time people reach the age of adulthood and approach marriage, they are so weighted down by cultural baggage and bad examples that they are ill-equipped to forge a lifetime union.

They still have a childish view of marriage and will not adopt a mature view until the childish one is set aside. Listen to the words of the apostle Paul:

Love never fails; but if there are gifts of prophecy, they will be done away: if there are tongues, they will cease; if there is knowledge, it will be done away. For we know in part, and we prophesy in part; but when the perfect comes, the partial will be done away. When I was a child, I used to speak as a child, think as a child, reason as a child; when I became a man, I did away with childish things. (1 Cor. 13:8-11)

THE REAL THING

Someone has said that the surest way to tell a straight stick is to lay a crooked stick up next to it. We have looked at a childish view of love—now let's examine the straight stick that is the real thing. If we're honest, the first aspect of real love that comes to mind is what the Greeks called *eros*: the passionate, physical expression of love. That is a part of marriage. Certainly if you are not ready to think in terms of erotic, sexual love as a part of the union of husband and wife, you are not ready to be married. But that is not usually the problem with *eros,* is it?

Our society is filled with the sensual. People do not subdue or downplay their desires as the Victorians once did; rather, these desires are broadcast, emphasized, expounded.

> *A lot of people have, before their marriage, replaced the real thing of* eros *with something that is not real at all.*

So why is it, then, that men and women today are finding the physical relationship of marriage less satisfying than ever? Bookshelves overflow with attention-getting titles like *Celibate Wives.* A glance at the *TV Guide* shows that Oprah, Phil, and Geraldo fill afternoon upon afternoon with talk of impotency, sexual frustration, and dysfunction. What has happened? Simply this: a lot of people have, before their marriage, replaced the real thing of *eros* with something that is not real at all.

In the fifties, a popular little song went something like this: "Oh, I'd rather have a paper doll to call my own, than have a fickle-minded, real live girl." In the fifties, it was nothing more than a cute, if silly, lyric. In the nineties, it bears a close resemblance to reality. Airbrushed images of modern day "paper dolls" may keep many men from having a relationship that is real and vital and dynamic with a flesh-and-blood, "real live girl." They have replaced reality with a kind of phony, synthetic relationship—a sure sign of immaturity and childishness.

For an uncut, unhyped view of *eros* in married love, no book beats the Bible. God's Word never backs away from the beauty and passion of sexual love. Read the Song of Solomon; if you're feeling really daring, read a modern translation. This is a beautiful story of a bride and groom who celebrated all the feelings involved in their union. If you have never read it, the sheer emotion may shock you. The picture of *eros* is pure and unde-filed—and it is glorious.

Eros, then, is an aspect of real love in marriage. But *philia,* the Greek word for "friend," is a second part of married love. I'm always a little put off by someone who says, "Oh, I could never marry him (her). We're just too good of friends." After all, I would strongly recommend that you marry someone who is your friend. Equally confusing to me are those who say, "I love him (her), but we're not what you would call friends." I married someone I could share with, talk to, go places with, confide in. I like to be with her, and she is my best friend.

Nearly 38 years ago this month, I picked up JoBeth for a date. I opened the car door for her and helped her in, then went around and got in on my side. Just as we left her house, I said, "JoBeth, I want to tell you something. I want you to know that I no longer like you as a girl friend." Silence. Just like I had planned it. I waited. She looked straight ahead and said nothing. After the appropriate dramatic pause I said, "JoBeth, I think I've fallen in love with you." You have never seen someone move across a car seat so fast. It's been many years since I made that statement, but I know this: I am in love with her, and I love her. And she is my friend like no other.

The third facet of real love is embodied in the Greek word *agape*. This kind of love only God possesses, and so, only He can give. *Agape* is a self-effacing, sacrificial kind of love that is exclusive, permanent, and unconditional. *Agape* love is essential to marriage because conditions in any relationship change. Health, outlook, financial status—all are subject to change. If love is to survive in an atmosphere of change, it must be rooted in something that is changeless.

I witnessed a television wedding recently that was "standard issue" in every way but one. The bride and groom were formally dressed. There were flowers, beautiful music, and family and friends in attendance. Rings were exchanged; vows were spoken—but with one slight variation. The bride and groom promised to "love and cherish, honor and sustain," but not as long as they both shall live. Oh no. These two promised to keep their vows as long as they both "shall love." Just one letter changes, but oh, what a difference that one letter makes.

> Agape *is a self-effacing, sacrificial kind of love that is exclusive, permanent, and unconditional.*

What they were saying is this: "Our love is conditional. It is for now, but it may not be for always. We'll have to see how we feel about it down the road. If the day should come when we stop loving each other, the deal is off. The commitment is no longer binding if we don't feel loving toward one another." That's a modern view of marriage—but it is a total misunderstanding of love.

Agape love is love that keeps its promises regardless of feeling or performance. It is love that acts—not on the basis of feeling, but on the basis of commitment. It holds itself to a vowed standard, trusting that feeling, when it is absent, will soon follow. It says, "I am going to act according to my promise. I will give myself sacrificially and unconditionally to this person, and we're going to make it work, believing that the romance, the feelings, the emotions are the fruit and not the anchor of our love." One writer said "the man who makes a vow makes an appointment with himself at some distant time or place."[2] *Agape* love intends to keep the appointment—and does so, regardless of circumstances.

HOW DO YOU KNOW?

If feelings do not define love, how can the real thing be discerned from its imposter? Those who are married have all been asked, "How did you know?" They can, and should, do better than answering, "When the right one comes, you'll know it too." Several practical characteristics can help to determine the real thing.

First, lovers want to be together. That should not surprise anyone. When my oldest son Ed was dating his wife Lisa, they wanted to be together all the time. The two of them would come over to our house and find some quiet spot to be alone and talk. When I would amble in to chat they would talk with me a while, then move on to another room where they could be alone—again. When they were not together, they liked to talk on the telephone—for long hours. Then when they could not talk on the phone, they wrote letters to one another.

One summer our family was in Jamaica, and Lisa wrote Ed long, long letters every day we were gone. We did not know what was going on at home—Ed was the only one getting regular mail—so he would get out the letters, read them, smile, nod, and put them away. Later he would take them out again. Same routine. Finally I said "Son, is there any news in there you'd like to read to your dad?" Although by this time I was certain he had memorized every word, he would always say, "I don't know, let me look." Then he would smile again and answer, "No, Dad, not a thing."

Lovers want to be together. They want to talk, to be alone, and to communicate with one another. That longing is one of the marks of real love.

Second, lovers see in their mate something special, something unique. My wife sees things in me that other people do not see. Lovers should see things in the ones they love that others do not see. John Newton, the sea-captain and slave trader who penned the hymn "Amazing Grace," proposed to Polly Catlett when he was 24 and she was 20. They had met when she was 13. Her family and friends objected to him, feeling that the two were such opposites that a marriage would be disastrous. She was unsure that she wanted to live the life of a sea-captain's wife, but she saw in him what no one else did: a brilliant mind. Although his education was limited, he was a voracious reader who taught himself the ancient languages and read Greek and Roman philosophers in his leisure time. She saw in him what no one else could see, and looked at him with what I call "love-washed eyes."

> *Lovers should see things in the ones they love that others do not see.*

When God looks at me, he sees Ed Young as a perfect person because the blood of Jesus Christ has cleansed me of my sin. God looks at me with "blood-washed eyes." He sees me as clean and whole and right because I am in Christ. That's the way God looks at every Christian, and in a sense, this is how every man or wife looks at his or her mate. They see the uniqueness in their mate and look at them with "love-washed eyes."

Third, when love is real, lovers want to commit themselves to one another. Jesus said, "Where your treasure is, there will your heart be also" (Matt. 6:21). Love is willing to commit to what it treasures.

> For always in love there is an immense and impossible decision to make, and there can be no real rest until it is made . . . love cannot circle around forever; it demands resoluteness, whole-hearted commitment. Never satisfied with just a little bit of a person's heart, love wants the whole thing, and is forever pushing toward the brink.[3]

When love is real, lovers are driven by it to commit to one another with loyalty, faithfulness, morality and fidelity. No one has to force them to the altar. They want to be there, and they choose to go.

THE SECRET TIME REVEALS
I have heard more jokes about marriage than I care to admit. I have seen grooms' cakes at wedding receptions that are topped with a ball and chain. I have watched nervous grooms teased unmercifully by groomsmen about being "captured," and heard marriage referred to as an institution not unlike prison. I was scared to death at my own wedding, and remember thinking, *I wonder what I'm really getting into?* But there is a secret to marriage that only time reveals. If you have been married only briefly, you will not have discovered this. And if you have never married, you may have trouble believing it because of all the myths that surround marriage today.

The road to marriage begins when two people say they have "fallen in love." Perhaps the expression is appropriate, because it hints at something dramatic. Even as the process of love unfolds over time, there is drama, a sense of importance. "In love" implies a circle—something that contains the two of you and closes you in. You are together in your love, separate from all others. So one stage you could call "falling in love," and another could be termed "being in love."

Then there is the stage of loving. All three stages are wonderful and are part of courtship and marriage.

The secret you should know is this: As you are married through the years, you can keep on falling in love—over and over again. If you have never known a successful marriage, this is a revolutionary idea. If you have never been married, it may surprise you. But every time you fall in love again with your mate, the love gets deeper and deeper, better and better, and more mature in every way.

I know what it means to fall in love, and fall again. I know what it means to be in love, and to love, and it's tremendous. You might say "Pastor, you've been lucky." But luck is not enough. Real love involves letting go of childish ideas and expectations of love, giving up reliance on feelings, and living out love on the basis of commitment. Circumstances change, but real love steps to the line, over and over again.

As you are married through the years, you can keep on falling in love—over and over again.

I know of a couple who have been married over fifty years. They have three grown children and two grandchildren. He is a retired civil servant, in excellent health, who loves to golf and plays as often as he can. She suffers from Parkinson's disease and her condition deteriorates almost daily. A few years ago she suffered a stroke that has altered her personality and limited her physical capabilities, causing her to require constant care and supervision. In appearance and in nature she has changed greatly from the wife she once was.

Last Thanksgiving this couple ate dinner at their daughter's home. He helped her with her food, as he has for some time. After dinner the table was cleared for coffee and dessert. When her pie was served, she immediately—to her daughter's alarm—turned it off her plate and onto the table, and tried to eat it. He calmly brushed aside their attempts to clean up the mess; instead he slid his own dessert onto the table as well, smiled, patted her hand reassuringly, and topped both his dessert and hers with a big dollop of whipped cream!

It is easy to know the real thing when you see it, isn't it? No spot is better suited for love and romance than the home, and there is no reason why couples should be satisfied to simply "beat the odds" by avoiding divorce. No one goes to the altar in marriage with the hope that their union will be average or ordinary. As G. K. Chesterson said:

> The thing which keeps life romantic and full of fiery possibilities is the existence of these great plain limitations which force all of us to meet the things we do not like or do not expect.[4]

Married or never-married, single, separated or divorced, the question is the same: Do you have a marriage that sizzles? Do you desire one? The difficult things that are blamed for making marriage fail are the very things that can, in fact, make it sizzle. The choice is yours.

Questions for Further Reflection

1. How did you make the decision to marry your spouse? What things influenced your decision? What things have confirmed it?

2. Do you believe it is possible to keep on falling in love with your mate? Why or why not?

3. What qualities do you recognize in your mate that others may not see? If you have not told your mate how you appreciate these things, do so today! (Better still, tell someone else what you appreciate about him or her.)

2

WHY MARRIAGES FIZZLE

I LIKE TO THINK OF MARRIAGE AS A private castle. The definition fits the institution well, I believe. The word "private" means secluded, not for common use. It implies something out of the public view. Marriage should be a private, exclusive enterprise that is secluded from the world in much the same way that a castle might be surrounded by a moat. The biblical account of the first marriage describes this kind of private intimacy:

> And the LORD God fashioned into a woman the rib which he had taken from the man. . . And the man said, "This is now bone of my bones, and flesh of my flesh; she shall be called Woman, because she was taken out of Man." For this cause a man shall leave his father and his mother, and shall cleave to his wife; and they

shall become one flesh. And the man and his wife were both naked and were not ashamed (Gen. 2:22-24).

Words like "cleave," "one flesh," "naked," and "not ashamed" bear witness to the private nature of marriage.

THREATS TO MARRIAGE

A castle is a place of refuge, a protected place. Its walls give security to its inhabitants and keep its detractors outside. Sometimes castles come under attack, and if there is any structure in our culture today that I would describe as "under attack," it would be the private little castle of marriage. Once marriage was respected and protected by society as a whole, but that day is gone. Today every marriage, as well as the institution of marriage itself, is under attack.

Hostile Attack

A subtle undercurrent in our secular society threatens to redefine marriage completely. The Genesis account of Adam and Eve demonstrates that God's view of marriage is one man with one woman—for life. An Austin, Texas, newspaper shocked a few readers, but apparently not a majority, by running an engagement photo of two lesbians in its wedding pages recently. A former Mr. Universe married another male body builder in a church ceremony presided over by a Unitarian minister and celebrating their homosexual union. This couple even had a formal period of engagement and showers prior to their wedding, and they have since marketed a video intended to help teenagers accept homosexuality as a healthy lifestyle choice. A well-known Hollywood couple have cohabited for a decade, have a "yours, mine, and ours" household of

The sacred relationship of marriage as ordained by God is under hostile attack from without—and the invasion is well underway.

children, refer to each other publicly as "husband" and "wife," yet have never legally wed.

Not only is the "one man with one woman" aspect of marriage under attack, the idea of marriage for life is no longer seen as essential. The popularity of pre-nuptial agreements, referred to by attorneys as "divorce agreements," indicates the lack of commitment with which many marriages begin. So the sacred relationship of marriage as ordained by God is under hostile attack from without—and the invasion is well underway.

Friendly Fire

Marriages are also threatened today by what I call friendly fire. This threat occurs when a door or window to the private little castle of marriage is left open, and family, friends, and neighbors are allowed to enter in. This form of attack is indirect, but it can do enormous damage to the "one flesh" aspect of any marriage. Almost without exception I believe it is a mistake to open up a marriage to the inspection of non-professional outside parties—especially relatives. I have seen too many husbands and wives struggle with one another and then call in a best friend, aunt, uncle, cousin, mother-in-law or father-in-law, sister or brother who becomes hopelessly entangled in their domestic affairs. Often any chance of reconciliation is killed, and there is great embarassment in having exposed the intimacies of the marriage to others.

> *Intrusion by others, well-meaning though they may be, can destroy the oneness God intends you to have with your mate.*

A father believes that no man is worthy of his daughter. He gives her away at the altar, but in his heart he says, "If he so much as blinks an eye. . . ." A mother loves her son and knows no girl is fine enough for her boy. Let marital conflict begin, and she is there defending the turf of her son. And in his mother the son finds a sympathetic, willing ear. Intrusion by others, well-meaning though they may be, can destroy the oneness God intends you to have with your mate. As you or I begin to share what happens in the secret, secluded, private castle of our marriage with others, we make a grave mistake.

Behind the Lines Invasion   A marriage experiences "behind the lines invasion," when the childish nature of a man or woman becomes apparent over time and permeates the relationship. All people have some "child" left in them. Pride, jealousy, anger, and resentment are childish responses that do not magically disappear at the legal age of adulthood. However, the intense, daily intimacy of marriage exposes childishness. Mike Mason, in his book *The Mystery of Marriage*, says marriage is "far more engrossing than we want it to be. It always turns out to be more than we bargained for. It is disturbingly intense, disruptively involving, and that is exactly the way it was designed to be. It is supposed to be more, almost, than we can handle."[1]

So when your private castle of marriage is infiltrated by the childishness of its own inhabitants, don't despair. Remember, only fairy tales promise pure happiness. Marriage is earthly, but glorious work.

BUILDING THE HOUSE   Years ago, the unmarried apostle Paul wrote a description of the hierarchy, the building of a marriage, that is as practical as it is beautiful. "But I want you to understand," he said, "that Christ is the head of every man, and the man is the head of the woman, and God is the head of Christ" (1 Cor. 11:3). Suppose a couple decides to build a house. The wife goes out and hires an architect, a contractor, and an interior decorator for good measure. The husband gets another architect, another contractor, another decorator. Everyone shows up at the same time, on the same lot—ready to build the house. Would you anticipate any problems during the construction of this new residence?

Of course they might compromise. Sometimes that is possible. She wants the room pink. He likes yellow. Maybe they could paint it half pink and half yellow—or decide on a color that is the first choice of neither of them. But wouldn't it be a lot better if they started with the same architect? The same contractor? The same decorator? Can you imagine the advantages of having a single set of plans? In marriage, you and your mate are trying to build not a house, but a home that God can honor. Your marriage is a private castle that is sacred, sheltered, and secluded—and under the care and authority of the Lord of the manor, whose name is Jesus Christ.

Security

Dr. Ed Wheat, in his book *Intended for Pleasure*, talks about the need for stability, security, and serenity in marriage. If you and I were to build a model of the private castle that is marriage, the walls would represent security. Without security there is no real intimacy, no honesty, and little trust. Walls keep that which is inside, inside, and that which is outside, outside. That is their function, what they were designed to do.

A few years ago, educators were very high on a classroom and teaching style known as "the open concept." In the open concept, the classroom walls came down and children were taught in a large, spacious environment with clustered learning centers and groups. Teachers, by and large, gave the plan a zero. Why? Noise was difficult to control. Other children and their teachers, now visible because the walls had been removed, became a serious distraction. What was meant to provide a free and unrestricted learning experience actually delivered insecurity and a lack of focus.

> *"Open marriage" is an oxymoron. . . . Marriage is meant to be completely and unapologetically closed.*

The open concept has been proposed by some soci-
ologists and psychologists in marriage, too, but "open
marriage" is an oxymoron. Marriage is exclusionary by
definition. It is meant to be completely and unapolo-
getically closed.

> . . . Anyone who enters into marriage actually relin-
> quishes the right to engage in any other adult relation-
> ship which might be equally deep or pervasive. One
> chooses one's mate as one chooses one's God: forsaking
> all others, until death.[2]

This intentional exclusivity builds a wall of security
around the marriage and its partners: two enter into
their private little castle; no others enter, and no one
leaves.

Stability If, in our model of marriage, the walls represent security, the joining of the walls represents stability. The
walls of a home are not simply propped up; they are put
together with nails or mortar or glue so that they can
withstand the pressures from without and within.

Texas weather is notoriously unpredictable, especially in Houston. Visitors are often told that if the
weather is not to their liking, another day could make
a world of difference, and I have found that to be true.
Last summer the western edge of our city was struck by
several severe storms over a period of hours. Tornadoes
are usually thought of as a midwestern phenomenon,
but twisters touched down in several spots that day,
including a rather exclusive neighborhood of estate
homes worth hundreds of thousands of dollars. The
damage was unbelievable. Roofs missing. Brick fences
reduced to rubble. Windows blown out. Trees toppled.
Even these well-built homes did not escape serious
damage, but they stood. Can you imagine the scene if
the walls of these homes were not well-reinforced?

What if they were not held together at their joints by something solid?

What is the stuff that gives marriage stability at its seams? It is the plan—the operating instructions—from the Maker of marriage whose name is God. He designed the home to be a theocracy where the Lord Jesus Christ is in charge and His rule book is heeded. In an unstable home there is no plan, or God's plan is ignored.

> *God designed the home to be a theocracy where the Lord Jesus Christ is in charge and His rule book is heeded.*

In a patriarchy, for example, the man is the dictator of the family. Picture Baron Von Trapp from *The Sound of Music*. He blew a whistle and children came running, lining up from tallest to smallest and briskly barking out their names on cue. His household was orderly without, but utterly chaotic within, as nanny and housekeeper Maria soon discovered. In a matriarchy, the woman is the CEO of the family—calling the shots, making the decisions, and using all the beguilements at her disposal to assure everyone that she is in charge. Neither of these all-too-common scenarios is God's plan.

Nor is it His plan that no one is in charge, or that the children of a home are in charge—that is anarchy, and I believe it is the greatest tragedy of all for the family. The box office smash *Home Alone* was a huge hit with the movie-going public, but real-life "home alone" cases are nothing less than tragic. Young children were never meant to fend for themselves or to manage the affairs of a home while their parents are at work or play.

Patriarchy, matriarchy or the-children-are-in-charge anarchy all spell an unstable home. Stability results from adherence to God's plan, and it is essential to withstand the internal and external forces that threaten marriage and family today.

Serenity   Finally, no home is built without a roof. The roof is the crown of the private little castle of marriage, and it represents serenity. Calm and peaceful, the home should be the one place where people are certain they will be welcomed, received, protected, and loved. I know men and women who use the office or the gym or the local watering hole as a pseudo-home to avoid the conflict or hostility of "the real thing." How sad! JoBeth has made our home a place of warmth and refuge—and I look forward to the serenity of it day after day, year after year. Charlie Shedd, whose wonderful wife Martha was the inspiration behind his many books on love and marriage, described his anticipation at coming home each day:

> *Calm and peaceful, the home should be the one place where people are certain they will be welcomed, received, protected, and loved.*

When I drive home in the evening, I must consciously guard the foot pedal, lest I step on the gas a little too fast as I approach the house where she waits for me. I still count it the biggest thrill when she comes hurrying from wherever she is to meet me, and, as I look down the road ahead, I see an elderly man and woman going into the sunset hand in hand.[3]

Shedd wrote these words after 26 years of married life. His vision of the future was an accurate one: Martha died peacefully in his arms after over half a century of married love.

Is your home a place of refuge that your mate longs for expectantly? Today more than ever, husbands and wives—and their children—need a home with a roof of serenity where they know they will be welcomed and warmed.

Some marriages begin well, then inexplicably, they fizzle. No major conflicts, no serious setbacks, just a realization one day like the message that sometimes comes across a television screen: *We have temporarily lost our signal; please stay tuned.* I believe that phrase could be used to describe a lot of marriages today. If they were honest about the state of their union, many couples would have to say, "We've lost the deep feelings we once had for each other. We don't know how or when, we just know that they are gone."

Has all the excitement and romance disappeared from your marriage? If it has, what happened? Maybe your signal has been "lost" for quite some time—and you've "stayed tuned," but the program has never resumed. You have a roommate, a legal contract, a partner. You may even have a divine covenant, but somehow you have lost the signal. It is just ho-hum. What happened?

Something about the dating relationship is explosive. It is passionate. It is exciting. Everything is new. Her eyes are a shade of green you have never seen before. His laugh is contagious and so distinctively different from anyone else's. The way she tilts her head your way in conversation is endearing. The way he navigates the confusing maze of gadgets in the hardware store is totally masterful. He/she is the most amazing creature you have ever met. How have you lived this long without him/her?

Then you marry. There is a honeymoon period, and the weeks become months, the months go into years, and somehow the years group themselves into decades. What used to be delightfully surprising is now deadeningly familiar. There is a comfort, to be sure, and an acceptance of one another that is charitable. But he/she is so ordinary. The "new" has worn off.

WE HAVE TEMPORARILY LOST OUR SIGNAL

Familiarity

If you are like me, when you get a new car, you want everything about it to be clean and perfect. You keep a list of all the little things that need adjusting, and you take it to the dealer to be worked on. The dog is not allowed in the car; the children can't drink Dr. Peppers in the back seat. Passengers must wear their seatbelts at all times. You keep the car washed and shiny, and you park as far from other cars as you can to avoid those irritating door dings that a new car seems to attract.

Then almost imperceptibly, your guard comes down. There is a rattle in the window, but you are used to it now. The dog is allowed riding privileges; a few Dr. Pepper cans litter the floorboard. You have stopped worrying about every little ding or noise. You let routine maintenance slide a bit, because, well, the new has worn off. The same thing is true with a new home or apartment. At first you want everything exactly right, but eventually—and you never really remember when—the "new" wears off and it is just another car, another house, another room.

Back in your courting years, you rang the doorbell right on time, gentlemen. Actually, you would have been early, but you circled the block a few times to avoid the appearance of being too eager. Ladies, you opened the door with a smile that said, "I've been waiting for this all day. I'm so glad you're finally here." You are sure your feet must have touched the sidewalk as you walked to the car, but you never felt it back then.

But after a few years of marriage, you come home 45 minutes late on a good day. You unlock the door with your own key, and are secretly relieved that it still works! You call out, "I'm home!" with a note of encouragement in your voice, and she shouts back, "I'm home, too! What did you expect, a hundred-piece marching band?"

Familiarity has set in. Both partners have begun to take one another for granted. What used to sizzle has now fizzled. I love the piece *The Saturday Evening Post* published many years ago called "The Seven Ages of the Cold." It chronicled the changes in marriage by tracing a husband's response to his wife's cold. It went something like this:

First year. The wife has a bad cold. The husband responds: "Sugar dumpling, I'm worried about my baby girl. You've got a bad sniffle. There's no telling about these things, with all this strep going around. I'm going to put you in the hospital this afternoon for a general check-up and a good rest. I know the food's lousy, but I'll bring you meals from Racini's. I've got it all arranged with the floor superintendent."

Second year. Bad cold. "Listen, darling, I don't like the sound of that cough. I've called Doc Miller to rush right over here. Now you go to bed like a good girl, just for poppa."

Third year. "Maybe you'd better lie down. Nothing like a little rest when you feel puny. I'll bring you something to eat. Have we got any soup?"

Fourth year. "Look, dear, be sensible. After you feed the kids and get the dishes washed, you'd better hit the sack. Ha, ha, ha."

Fifth year. "Why don't you just get up and take a couple of aspirin?"

Sixth year. "If you'll just gargle or something instead of sitting there, barking like a seal."

Seventh year. "For pete's sake, stop sneezing. What are you trying to do, give me pneumonia?"[4]

It is so easy through the years to allow the familiarity of marriage to dim real affection and concern. At the beginning spouses are attentive, eager to please, ready to help, ready to listen, willing to learn about one another. Then as the years go by the knowledge gained—the very same knowledge that could deepen their relationship—seems to cause their marriage to fizzle.

Fatigue   Fatigue is another strong but subtle weapon against the institution of marriage. Many people just get tired and stop working at it. Few would argue that they have more energy today in their thirties, forties, or fifties than they did in their newlywed teens or twenties. It is a good thing many of us did court and marry at a younger age—now we might not be able to muster the energy!

> *With age life becomes more—not less—complex. Responsibilities seem to multiply.*

Do you remember the days when you could go out five, six, seven evenings a week, stay out late each night, and manage to talk to your future spouse on the phone in between dates? I do. And the admission that I have not been able to maintain that pace for the last thirty-odd years should not come as a great surprise to anyone. With age our life becomes more—not less—complex. Responsibilities seem to multiply in the roles of husbands, wives, mothers, dads, sons, daughters, employers, employees, and friends.

Even church involvement can tap energy as people seek to serve God and use their spiritual gifts in the life of a body of believers. I tell people in our church family that if they are at church every time the doors are open they are making a big mistake. No one can do it all. It is futile to try—and to do so could be detrimental to the health of their marriages and family relationships.

> *There is no such thing as a no-maintenance marriage, but energy and time devoted to this holy enterprise will reap lasting, valuable dividends every time.*

When the competing time demands of running a home or a business, raising children, travel, hobbies, recreation and friends begin to close in from every side, most people often neglect what should be their number one priority: their mate. They rationalize: *He/she knows I love him/her. I'll devote more time to our relationship when this project/program/trip/season is over.*

And they put off spending their energy, passion, and interest on the one person who should be first in line while everyone and everything else waits.

If you are too tired to love your wife or your husband, and to expend the energy it takes to nurture a relationship as vital as your marriage, you are too tired, period. Too many couples assume that their marriage runs like a small appliance: plug it in and walk away. No maintenance necessary. There is no such thing as a no-maintenance marriage, but energy and time devoted to this holy enterprise will reap lasting, valuable dividends every time.

WHAT IF IT IS JUST NOT WORKING?

Maybe your marriage is in trouble today. You would be relieved to think it has just fizzled; you are actually afraid it may have already burned out. If that is the case, you have some choices before you. You could choose divorce. I am not advocating this choice, but there is no arguing the fact that millions of Americans each year see this as the only way out. You could decide that you have had it and simply quit.

A talented Bible teacher in our congregation married for the first time later in life. Her husband was a widower and a fine Christian man who courted and won this lovely lady with determination, patience, and kindness. She recounts that at their wedding she made many lofty promises and thought she knew this man she stood beside inside and out.

After being married to him for some time, she realized that all she truly knew on her wedding day was that she was promising not to quit. She could not know what the future would hold, or what the intimate crucible of marriage would reveal about herself or her mate. She acknowledges today she did not know enough then to promise life-long love or unending devotion. She simply promised not to quit.

When marriage seems to fizzle, divorce can look like the best solution. But it is usually the most immature choice available. And like this dear lady, it helps to remember that you promised not to quit.

If we renounce divorce as a choice when marriage is difficult or unsatisfying, what is left? Many couples would say they have chosen to "tough it out" instead. Legally they remain married, but in truth they live in separate, impenetrable worlds. When it is necessary or advantageous to present a united front they do so, but it is just that: a front. Then show time is over, and the two go back to their respective solitudes until the next command performance. This is a poor choice, too, although some might argue that it is preferable to divorce.

> *When a husband and wife decide to apply God's principles for marriage to their own union, they open themselves to endless possibilities for change.*

I am thankful there is a third option. When a husband and wife decide to apply God's principles for marriage to their own union, they open themselves to endless possibilities for change. Through love they can *build* an intimate marriage—a marriage that sizzles. They should decide for themselves that regardless of the decision or response of their mate, they are going to try it God's way. When a husband and a wife both make this choice, they are at a good beginning place, no matter how old or new the marriage may be. But it is only a beginning. That one-time decision is not a cure-all for a marriage that has only limped along for years. They must now be willing to commit themselves to the task ahead, and that involves work.

Dr. James Dobson, popular author and host of "Focus on the Family," tells the story of how his mother attended an Oklahoma high school in the 1930s that had not won a single football game in six years. Every Friday night for those six years, the local team just got the stew beat out of them. If you're not from Texas or

Oklahoma, let me tell you that high school football is big league stuff in this neck of the woods. Losing every time began to get old, and eventually, people didn't want to go to the games. They looked for any excuse not to have to watch what had, by this time, become certain defeat.

After yet another Friday night loss, a wealthy oil tycoon went into the locker room and gave a pep talk unlike any other since Knute Rockne. He said, "Folks, I'm going to make you a promise. If you'll win the football game next Friday night, I'll give every coach and every boy on this team a brand new Chevrolet." He'd made a lot of money in the early thirties in the oil boom, and every person in the room knew he could make good on his promise. The excitement was electric. The atmosphere was more like a Super Bowl victory party than a perpetually losing locker room.

The players were incredulous: "You mean, if we beat them next week—"

"That's right," the oilman said.

"Every one of us will get his own car?"

"Absolutely."

The excitement in that room spilled over to the school and the entire community. Those players could see themselves riding around in Chevy coups with the prettiest girls in school. The coaches pictured them-selves leaving practice in *their* new cars and imagined the envy of "less fortunate" coaches from other schools. All week, the entire campus buzzed. Practices had an intensity that had never been matched. The coaches strategized endlessly. The players listened more atten-tively than ever before. Finally, game day arrived. The coach stood up in the locker room prior to the kickoff and uttered some forgetable, inane words about how important this contest was, as if anyone was unsure. The team took the field with a roar. Adrenaline was at an all-time high. Yet at the end of four, hard-fought quarters of football, they had lost again—by a score of 38-0.

What happened? Just this: You cannot, in one week, make up for a lack of training, a lack of instruction, a lack of commitment, and a lack of enthusiasm that has been entrenched for years. No matter how motivated you are, a week is not enough time to overcome a defeatist mentality.

Making your marriage sizzle—breathing new life into an enterprise that was close to death—will take time. Start today by making a commitment as a husband or as a wife to putting God's precepts into practice in your home. And one day, you will wake up in a home that has more grace, more love, and more excitement than either of you would have ever dreamed possible.

QUESTIONS FOR FURTHER REFLECTION

1. What do you see as the greatest general threat to marriages today? Is it an issue in your marriage?

2. What is the greatest threat your own marriage faces?

3. What steps are you and your mate prepared to take to safeguard your marriage? Discuss them, and, if possible, set them in place now.

4. In what ways has your relationship become predictable? Plan a surprise for your mate this week—or agree to try something together that is new to both of you.

PART TWO

PREPARING THE KINDLING

3

AIM AT
SOMETHING!

"BY THE AUTHORITY VESTED IN ME, by the laws of the State of Texas, and looking to heaven for divine sanction, I now pronounce you husband and wife, in the presence of God and these assembled witnesses."

These words are spoken by the ministers of our church to nearly two hundred couples each year. Every time I say them, I get a lump in my throat. I can truthfully say that I am more nervous presiding over a wedding ceremony before a handful of people than I am preaching before hundreds of folks. The seriousness and the sacredness of those moments before God—the beauty of the spoken vows, and the miracle of two becoming one flesh overwhelms me every time.

Two young people come together in marriage, and out of their union, other lives will come into being that would never have been had these two not joined their lives. As a minister, I tell them that they are promising to be together for the rest of their lives: "until death do you part." But that unseen future parting seems so far away at the marriage altar, so foreign to the joy of the moment. "In sickness and in health," they promise, thinking perhaps of colds or flu—hardly understanding the depth of a vow that binds still in permanent disability, or even when one no longer recognizes the other. "In poverty and in wealth" they agree to stand together, not forseeing the day when one spouse, perhaps, risks their nest egg on a sure investment only to lose every penny they have saved.

When a man and woman come together and say "I do" to these vows, no wonder mothers and daddies cry, grandparents bite their lips, bridesmaids' knees shake, and the best man's palms sweat. This is serious, sacred, awesome stuff. Then the words, "I now pronounce you husband and wife. . . What God has joined together let no man put asunder" come, and the two kiss, turn, face friends and family, and take the first steps of their new life together.

It's a dangerous proposition, a tremendous risk. I think about the girls I dated and thought at times that I might marry, and I remember praying, "Oh, help her to like me," or "Let her want to marry me." I thank God that He in His wisdom did not affirmatively answer those early prayers.

So many single adults see marriage as *the* great goal of life. Then they meet someone they choose to marry and imagine that they have somehow "arrived," only to find that marriage in and of itself is an unworthy goal. If marriage is the goal, what do you do for the rest of your life after you've attained it?

A young medical student was given a tour of the hospital where he would train in the future. A resident led him into a semi-private room where two men were situated. The student spoke to both of them, but neither responded. One of them did not even look up. As the student left the room, he queried the resident: "What's wrong with them?" The resident replied, "Well, the guy in bed number one is in good health physically, but he was in love with this girl—they dated, were engaged, and he was head over heels about her. At the last minute, she ditched him for another man. Now he doesn't talk to anyone. He's in severe depression and refuses to communicate."

> *If just getting married and being married are the only goals you have, you're in for a disappointment.*

"I see," said the med student. "What about the other guy—the one in bed number two? He seems almost as bad. Did he lose his girl, too?"

"Him? Oh, no," the resident countered, "he's the one that got her."

The moral of this little story is simple: You can get in big trouble married; you can get in big trouble not married. Marriage is not the panacea many believe it to be.

GOAL SETTING

If just getting married and being married are the only goals you have, you're in for a disappointment. Every problem or shortcoming a single person has will be amplified, underscored, italicized in marriage. When psychologists list life events that increase stress, marriage rates very high on the scale. Mike Mason writes,

> Marriage, even under the very best of circumstances, is a crisis . . . and it is a dangerous thing not to be aware of this. Whether it turns out to be a healthy, challenging and constructive crisis or a disastrous nightmare depends largely upon how willing the partners are to be changed, how malleable they are. [1]

Marriage is not an end. It is a beginning. It is not a destination; it is a method of travel. I am always amazed when I ask a nearly or newly married couple about goals. Nine times out of ten, he will look at her, she will look at him, then they'll both shrug their shoulders and look at me! "We don't know," they may answer, or "What do you mean by goals?" Certainly I could not presume to prescribe goals for your marriage. Yours would be different from mine and from those set by other couples. But I can tell you this: you'd better have some. The old maxim is true: Aim at nothing and you'll hit it every time.

Retired General Norman Schwarzkopf, in discussing the principles that guided him to victory in the Persian Gulf, pointed to the necessity of goal-setting. "You must have clear goals. And you must be able to articulate them clearly. One of the advantages we had in Kuwait," he said, "was the clarity of the mission: Kick Saddam Hussein. . . out of Kuwait. The goal was clear and simple, and something that every one of our troops understood."[2]

> *People need simple, clear, straightforward, and easily understood goals if they are to reach their desired destination in marriage.*

That's war, you might argue. This is marriage. And marriage is under attack, so perhaps the same advice would apply, after all. People need simple, clear, straightforward, and easily understood goals if they are to reach their desired destination in marriage. The problem with most goals set for marriage, however, is that they are what I would call "negative goals."

Avoid Negative Goals

For example, a young man was reared in a family that was in a constant state of conflict. Any time the family got together, strife, bedlam, and verbal abuse were the order of the day. They would sit down for a meal and it was almost a contest to see who could offend the most, who could challenge, who could attack, or who could hurt another family member with the harshest words. The table became a battlefield, and every family member was a mercenary soldier out for blood.

When this young man married, he had one goal for his marriage and family. You can guess what it was, I'm sure. "We are never going to fight in my family. There will never be a disagreement. No cross words. My home will be completely free of conflict, and we will never get into arguments with one another." What do you think happened as a result of that negative goal? There was conflict, of course, because when more than one person inhabits a home, conflict is inevitable. It didn't go away. It just went underground.

I'm always wary when I hear a couple tell me they have never had a cross word. Sometimes I wonder if they ever have a word at all. Years ago when I pastored a church in Canton, North Carolina, I voiced that suspicion from the pulpit. On that particular Sunday morning, a woman walked out the door with husband in tow, and dragged him over to me. She was a pit bull of a woman, and her eyes blazed as she said, "Preacher, you have told something that is not true today. We've been married forty-eight years and we stand here as a testimony. We have never had a cross word in all our years of marriage. Isn't that right, L.L.?"

Knowing his cue, L.L. replied, "That's right, preacher, never a cross word." His name, by the way, was "Little Love." And quite literally, that was what he had known in his 48-year marriage: little love and almost total domination. And I still believe that any couple who says they have never argued is either lying or one partner is totally dominating the other.

> *It is unrealistic to think that any marriage will be conflict-free. To make the absence of conflict a marital goal is self-defeating.*

It is unrealistic to think that any marriage will be conflict-free. To make the absence of conflict a marital goal is self-defeating. Conflict will come—and if your goal is to avoid it, there will be a cost involved. Issues can be avoided and ignored for so long, but eventually the emotions that have been stuffed beneath the surface will explode, then guilt will ensue. The partners will pray: "Oh, Lord, forgive us. Our goal was never to have conflict, and we've failed." Negative marital goals always fall short. Perhaps a better goal would be to learn to deal with conflict as Christians in a way that is not damaging to one another.

Set Positive Goals The best place to begin to set goals in marriage is with the partner whose shortcomings you know best: yourself. I would encourage husbands and wives to spend some time alone and develop a list of things about themselves they would like to see change. Write "What I Would Like to Change About Myself" at the top of the page, and begin.

> *The best place to begin to set goals in marriage is with the partner whose shortcomings you know best: yourself.*

Then, start to think about your partner. Take another piece of paper and title it "What I Would Like to Change About My Mate." When you're done, take a deep breath, pray for wisdom and humility, and exchange lists with your spouse. If you have teenagers and you are exceptionally brave, ask them what they think is good about their home and what they feel could be improved. Consider looking at those lists, too.

ACHIEVING YOUR GOALS Now you have the basis for some realistic marital goals. Set some priorities, pray over them, and begin the work that it will take to make progress in each area. Your union will be stronger and more satisfying for the effort. As you and your mate pursue these agreed-upon goals, I believe three things will help you achieve them: commitment, character, and the willingness to change.

Commitment means that when you marry, you are able to say, "I am totally, unreservedly, without any qualification or hesitation whatsoever, committed to this man or this woman, till death do us part, so help me God." Men, if there is any other way for you to love a woman short of marriage, if your love for her is satisfied with anything less than a total surrender of your life, love her that way—don't marry her. Women, do not marry a man you are not willing to follow—not just into marriage, but into any situation your future together might hold. If there is the slightest hesitation on your part about whether you can do this—don't marry him.

Commitment: The "C" Word

Garry Friesen explores this concept in *Decision Making and the Will of God:*

> It would be wise for a man, for instance, to select a woman toward whom he could most easily and completely fulfill his commitments as a husband. A woman, observing that Scripture requires her to submit to her husband, should be asking in advance, "For what kind of man would submission come easily?," and so on.[3]

This kind of radical commitment is not forged in a vacuum. It involves community and family and church. The wonderful thing about a husband and wife being a part of the body of Christ is that it provides so much support for their marriage. Christian friends offer encouragement and provide fellowship. Biblical principles undergird the workings of the home and offer

Wherever your marriage is today, make or reaffirm your unyielding commitment to its permanence.

guidance in times of uncertainty or struggle. I believe divorce was a very rare thing when I was young, in part because marriage was begun with deep commitment and that commitment was actively supported by the church and by the families of those who wed.

Wherever your marriage is today, make or reaffirm your unyielding commitment to its permanence. Ruth Bell Graham, wife of evangelist Billy Graham, was once asked whether she had ever considered divorce. "Murder, yes," she jokingly replied. "Divorce, never." Commitment is where marriage begins.

The Quest for Character

Francis and Edith Schaeffer first met one another at a Sunday evening meeting featuring a speaker whose topic was "How I Know That Jesus Is Not the Son of God and How I Know the Bible Is Not the Word of God." They were the first two on their feet to challenge him as he completed his presentation, each thinking they were probably the only one in the room who might make a defense for the claims of Christ. Francis argued first, then Edith stood and spoke. After the meeting concluded, he approached the young girl whose words had impressed him:

"May I take you home?" he asked.

"I'm sorry. I already have a date," she responded.

"Break it," he told her.

She did, and a courtship ensued that ended in marriage. It began with a mutual admiration of that elusive quality we know as character. I believe character is the most important quality anyone can seek to find in a husband or wife. How do you recognize character? First Corinthians chapter 13 describes character as it relates to love.

Love is patient. It would be difficult, would it not, to live with an impatient person? (My wife says it can be, for a fact.)

Love is kind. Is the person you love truly kind? Considerate? Are you?

Love is not jealous, is not possessive. I talked recently with a wife who said her husband was convinced she was having an affair with the meter reader. "He is so possessive of me," she said "that I am a virtual prisoner in my own home." To live in a relationship where there is no trust is to live in bondage.

Love does not brag, is not arrogant. Those who appear to be the most arrogant and self-assured are often the most insecure. Imagine the constant drain of living with someone who must continually be "propped up" or reassured! True character does not call attention to itself; it can let its weaknesses be known, as well as its strengths.

Love does not act unbecomingly, does not seek its own. This is selfishness. How giving are you? How giving is your mate? Are either of you difficult if things do not go your way?

Love is not provoked. How many times have you heard someone excuse this character flaw by saying "I can't help it when I fly off the handle. I've just got a bad temper"? Real character exhibits self-control.

Does not rejoice in unrighteousness. Are you married to someone who is always negative? About everything? It would be extremely difficult to live day in and day out with someone who constantly scrutinized you and let you know (with enthusiasm) that you seldom measured up.

Are you a person of character? Does your life mirror the attributes of genuine love outlined by Paul in this familiar passage? Are the fruits of the spirit—love, joy, peace, patience, kindness, goodness, gentleness, self-control—in evidence in your life? In your spouse's life? If these attributes are, they will form the basis for trust in your relationship, and enrich the soil of your marriage so that growth can occur.

> *Nothing so limits a marriage as the desire to make a snapshot out of what should be a moving picture.*

Nothing so limits a marriage as the desire to make a snapshot out of what should be a moving picture. A   *The Willingness to Change*

marriage that never changes may as well be over and
done. "Grow old along with me," wrote Robert Browning, "the best is yet to be; the last of life, for which the
first is made . . . ."[4] The often quoted seven last words
of the church, "We've never done it that way before,"
apply to far too many marriages, also. My head spins
when I think of the changes JoBeth and I have seen in
the years we have shared together. No children. Then a
son, then two, then three. Our first left home, then the next, and the
last. Again, just the two of us. The delight of grandchildren. New cities, new challenges, new friends. . . and in the midst of it all, contentment.

> *The secret of contentment in the midst of change is found in having roots in the changeless Christ—the same yesterday, today and forever.*

The apostle Paul said, "I know
how to get along with humble means, and I also know
how to live in prosperity; in any and every circumstance
I have learned the secret of being filled and going
hungry, both of having abundance and suffering need"
(Phil. 4:12). The secret of contentment in the midst of
change is found in having roots in the changeless
Christ—the same yesterday, today, and forever. The
courage to change—the willingness to change—will
enable a husband and wife to take the lists each has
made, exchange them, and say, "If the person who
knows me best—my best friend, my lover, and my
mate—would say this about me, then I'm going to take
it seriously. By the grace of God and with the help of
my spouse, I'm going to work at changing to make my
marriage even better."

Leonard Ravenhill offers this list of questions for the
man or woman serious about becoming all that God
would have him or her to be. They are worthwhile for
a husband or wife to consider regularly, with a heart
willing to make whatever changes the Holy Spirit
prompts:

Am I consciously or unconsciously creating the impression that I am a better man than I really am? Is there the least suspicion of hypocrisy in my life? Am I honest in all my words and acts? Do I exaggerate? Am I reliable? Can I be trusted? Do I confidentially pass on what was told to me in confidence? Do I grumble or complain in the church? Am I jealous, impure, irritable, touchy, distrustful? Am I proud? Do I thank God that I am not as other people? Is there anyone I fear or dislike or criticize or resent? If so, what am I doing about it?

Before you rush to test your mate with this list, read on:

What about my devotion to God? Does the Bible live to me? Do I give it time to speak to me? Do I go to bed on time and get up on time? Am I enjoying my prayer life today? Did I enjoy it this morning? When I am involved in a problem in life, do I use my tongue or my knees about it? Am I disobeying God in anything, or insisting upon doing something about which my conscience is uneasy? When did I last speak to someone else with the object of trying to win that person to Christ? Am I a slave to books, dress, friends, work, or convention? How do I spend my spare time?[5]

STAYING ON TRACK

Herman Miller Inc. manufactures office and health care facility furniture and is consistently recognized as one of the best managed companies in the United States. Herman Miller's CEO, Max DePree, is the author of the best selling *Leadership Is an Art* and *Leadership Jazz*, and his unconventional but effective management practices have made the company the focus of national and international acclaim. Their tremendous sales performance—increasing from $50 million in 1976 to over $850 million today—is a surefire attention-getter, too.

What makes Herman Miller Inc. a success? One thing: clearly stated values are supported and understood at every level. Virtually everyone in the company, from furniture assemblers to executives, can articulate the firm's philosophy and its goals. And an infrastructure has been allowed to develop that encourages open, honest communication, regardless of organizational rank or responsibility. There is no fear of retribution for calling someone "three levels up" with an idea or a problem.

Employees are encouraged to challenge the status quo—and to find a better way of doing things. Honesty is valued, and so is hard work. "It sounds syrupy," says one senior vice president, "but the major thing that's helped us is that we've always focused on doing what is morally right to do, not what is expedient."[6] An annual employee survey is undertaken to identify processes and policies that need to be changed and to address business conditions that may be keeping the company from meeting its stated goals.

> *What do you think might happen in a marriage partnership where the "key stockholders" set equally high goals for their union, cultivated communication, and put a high premium on "doing the right thing?"*

What is it like to work in a place where goals are high, communication is prized and people really care about one another? HMI's absentee rate is between 1 and 2 percent—well below the industry standard of 6 percent. Employee turnover at 7 percent is less than half of the 15 to 20 percent average of other U.S. firms.

What do you think might happen in a marriage partnership where the "key stockholders" set equally high goals for their union, cultivated communication, and put a high premium on "doing the right thing"? I think it might be as big an attention-getter in our culture as a company like Herman Miller Inc. Just like HMI executives give ownership away for the good of the enterprise, husbands and wives have to realize that they do not "own" their marriage. It is God's enterprise. In fact, as believers, they do not even own the rights to themselves, do they? They all have been bought and paid for with a price and are called to glorify God with all that they have and all that they will ever be.

When conditions test your union and decisions affecting its direction must be made, imagine that a board meeting convenes among the "directors" of your life. Your emotions, your feelings, your memory, your logic and intellect, your will—all have stock to vote. A temptation or a test comes; the board meets. The chairman asks Feelings, "What do you think about this?"

"Well," Feelings replies, "it looks good to me. I think it will be gratifying—that it will give us tremendous pleasure. This kind of thing can produce a tremendous emotional high—and I'm all for that."

"Thank you, Feelings," the chairman responds. "What about you, Memory?

"Well, we've faced this thing before. Last time we struggled, then finally gave way, and things were fine for a while. Oh, there was some bitterness down the road, and we went through a time of sorrow, as I recall. Does everyone remember?"

"Fine, Memory, that will be all. Logic and Intellect, let's hear from you."

"Yes, well, there are six or seven ways to go with this, of course. We could say yes. We could say no. We could say maybe. Or we could postpone any decision until we have more information. We could say we're exploring other options, of course; that is always an option. I would be happy to come up with a report that details all the possible responses and have it ready . . .

"Thank you, Logic and Intellect."

This is how the world makes choices, is it not? But in a corporation, and in a marriage, someone must ultimately make the call. Every board of directors has a chairman; in this case, the board is chaired by the will. And until the will is surrendered to God in Jesus Christ, it cannot be trusted to keep the enterprise on track.

It should come as no surprise, really, that the genius of a marriage that goes somewhere is direction and surrender. That means setting goals and then submitting to the leadership of God through His Word and His Holy Spirit. Remember your lists? Examine them now, and agree with your spouse what your goals for your marriage should be. Then when testing comes—and it will—resolve to rely not on your own strength or willpower or determination, but on God's strength and His leadership. He is more than able to complete what He has begun—and to do it well. Aim for something!

QUESTIONS FOR FURTHER REFLECTION

1. What do you and your mate want to accomplish during your next year of marriage? What about the next ten years? The next twenty-five?

2. If some of your marriage goals are "negative" (i.e., "we will not . . ."), work to restate them in positive terms.

3. How do you view change? Does your mate share your perspective? Set aside time to talk about the changes in your lives—both experienced and anticipated—and how you feel about them. What changes do you welcome as a couple? What changes do you fear?

4

A STRONG
WORD TO
WIVES

THERE MAY NOT BE A MORE CONTRO-
versial biblical passage for a pastor to preach from today
than Ephesians 5:22-24. It has been dismissed as ar-
chaic and anti-woman, the principle it teaches excluded
from modern marriage vows, and its practical truth
overshadowed by misunderstanding. But I believe that
its practice is essential to the success of any marriage
and that the wife who understands and heeds its charge
is a wise woman indeed.

Wives, be subject to your own husbands, as to the
Lord. For the husband is the head of the wife, as Christ
also is the head of the church, He Himself being the
savior of the body. But as the church is subject to
Christ, so also the wives ought to be to their husbands
in everything. (Eph. 5:22-24)

Why begin with this strong word to wives? Because I intend to follow with a stronger biblical word to husbands.

A lot of folks today argue with the biblical principles relating to marriage, saying, "I'm categorically against them—I don't agree." Yet they haven't even begun to understand what they dismiss. Others do understand, but say, "I choose not to believe. I choose not to practice those principles." The sad part of such a choice is simply this: God's way works. Not some of the time or even most of the time. God's way works all of the time. So people need to clearly understand His plan for man and woman in marriage, if for no other reason than because it works!

SETTING THE STAGE

To completely understand the apostle Paul's admonition to wives, consider the background in which his words were written. Beginning in verse 18 of the same chapter, he said, "Be filled with the [Holy] Spirit." Then he gave the characteristics, or the hallmarks, of a Spirit-filled life. If people are filled with the Holy Spirit, they will speak to one another in song—they will be positive, communicating, joyful people. They will sing, will make melody in their hearts. I'm reminded of that moment in musical after musical where you know the hero or the heroine or the cowboy is about to burst into song. If folks are filled with the Spirit, they are on the brink of a song all day long, and sometimes one will "spill over." In addition to speaking and singing, they will be thankful, appreciative, and full of gratitude for what God is doing in their lives. The final mark of the Spirit-filled life is found in verse 21—and that is *mutual submission*, one to another.

Before any word about submission was issued to the wife, Paul introduced the principle of mutual submission. It makes perfect sense, since we realize that every human being is made for relationship. People are constructed to be in relationship with other people. No one is created to be a stand-alone entity, an island, in and of himself. I cannot imagine a bleaker existence than to live with no interaction with others, surrounded by "I," "me," "my," and "mine" on every side. I am thankful that none is made that way.

> *I cannot imagine a bleaker existence than to live with no interaction with others, surrounded by "I," "me," "my," and "mine" on every side.*

People are created for relationship. For the Christian, the primary relationship in life is with the Lord Jesus Christ. The One who is Savior and Lord is to be the first priority and the deepest passion. If this is true of both parties in a marriage, when conflict arises there is a *third* presence, an ultimate authority to consult. "Be subject to one another in the fear of Christ," or in "the reverence of Christ," Paul wrote. This means when there is conflict or disagreement in marriage—because the wife's primary relationship is with Christ, and the husband's primary relationship is with Christ—this third party is to be considered by both "out of reverence."

Submission in marriage, then, is an act of reverence to Jesus Christ—not an issue of rights or privileges or "top dog" status. Husband and wife must be willing to abdicate their selfish claims and insistence on their own way out of reverence for Christ who is the Mediator—a go-between. In this context Paul introduced the operative word to wives in marriage—submission.

> *Submission in marriage is an act of reverence to Jesus Christ—not an issue of rights or privileges or "top dog" status.*

I do not know how many couples I have married in my years as a pastor, but only recently I have noticed more brides balking at the "s-word." "Could we skip that," some ask, "or change it to something else?" We could, I suppose, but I never do. The implications go far beyond semantics, and we attempt to alter the plan of God at our own risk! The world says submission is an unreasonable charge for women, that it relegates the wife to "doormat" status and second-class citizenship. Nothing could be further from the real truth.

When these words were first written, the church was in her infant stage and still greatly influenced by the Hebrew world—a world where women were treated as objects. When Jesus Christ preached and taught, he shattered prevailing prejudices and liberated many who were in bondage, but he elevated the status of none so dramatically, perhaps, as women. That Paul would write to the Galatian church "There is neither Jew nor Greek, there is neither slave nor free man, there is neither male nor female; for you are all one in Christ Jesus"(Gal. 3:28) was revolutionary. The Jew looked upon his wife as something he owned, and his laws allowed him to divorce her, almost at whim. Great controversy raged around the interpretation of this precept, found in Deuteronomy 24:1:

> When a man takes a wife and marries her, and it happens that she finds no favor in his eyes because he has found some indecency in her, and he writes her a certificate of divorce and puts it in her hand and sends her out from his house.

The phrase "some indecency" was the operative one. If a Jewish man could find some indecency in his wife, he could obtain two witnesses, have a rabbi write out a bill of divorcement, present her with it, and leave under the law. Eventually two schools of thought formed. Shammai, a very conservative rabbi, held that a man could divorce his wife for one cause only, and that was adultery. Only if a wife was guilty of adultery, he argued, did a man have grounds for divorce. Hillel, a more liberal teacher, held that "indecency" could be defined in much broader—and more trivial—terms. Indecency in Hillel's view could mean that a man's wife was seen speaking to another man in public. Or that she put too much salt on his food. Or burned his morning bagel, causing him to "find no favor with her."

This was the Jewish law of the day—and it did not favor women. The Greek world was even worse for the woman. The great Greek orator Demosthenes taught that courtesans were for recreation, concubines for daily cohabitation, and wives for the bearing of children, thus giving a man respectability. The Roman historian Jerome records a wedding ceremony that took place between a woman who had been married 24 times to her husband's 21—a record even Hollywood could not approach! In this atmosphere of decadence, immorality, and perversion, the woman was more often than not the victim of men.

> *The one place government cannot guarantee a woman the kind of respect and protection she deserves is not the workplace, the courtroom or the classroom—it is the home!*

"That's history," a modern female might argue. "Women have come a long way. We have rights. We have laws that protect us. We have freedom that we've never known before." But the one place government cannot guarantee a woman the kind of respect and protection she deserves is not the workplace, the courtroom, or the classroom—it's the home!

There is a way for a man and woman to live with one another in marriage that nurtures and protects them both, making their union strong and lasting. Two baseline requirements are presented in Scripture for this kind of partnership—one for the woman, and one for the man. And the baseline requirement for the woman in marriage is submission.

SUBMISSION AS AN OBLIGATION

Submission is a military word that means "to line up according to rank," or "to be under the authority of." A wife who is submissive to her husband is not saying in any way that she is inferior to him in intellect, wisdom, insight, or reason. The word relates more to function than status—and in the home, God places the weight of responsibility and accountability squarely on the shoulders of the husband.

Some women are probably already saying to themselves, "He doesn't know my husband. He won't make a decision. He's weak. He won't assert himself, and he won't lead. If I didn't take the lead with our children in church, about school, finances, etc., nothing would happen." I understand that there are men like that, and that some wives must act independently or chaos would reign. But if you are married to such a man, the minute he shows one ounce of initiative in any area, whatever that area might be—immediately submit to his leadership.

> *Marriage is not a business arrangement . . . It is a one-flesh relationship where both parties confer, fully expressing their opinions, ideas, and desires.*

Marriage is not a business arrangement where the husband holds 51 percent of the stock and the wife 49 percent. It is a one-flesh relationship where both parties confer, fully expressing their opinions, ideas, and desires. More often than not, there is agreement either initially or eventually, but when there is not, someone must make the call. This responsibility is the man's. And when the decision is made, the wife, if she is subject to her husband, supports that decision. Right or wrong, good or bad, she says, "I'm with you to the end. You've decided. I will follow." Then she does so fully and joyfully. That is submission.

My father and mother are both deceased. I would have to say, however, that my mother was the dominating force in the home in which I was reared. I can remember many times seeing my dad weigh decisions about this or that—about buying this house or borrowing a sum of money. But his word was not necessarily the final one. One time in particular he wanted to purchase a farm outside Laurel, Mississippi, where we lived. The little town was named Sandersville, and today it is the site of one of the only prominent oilfields in the state. When I was a little boy Dad wanted to buy a farm in Sandersville and was within $300 or so of having what he needed. My mother didn't want to do it, and we didn't. The man who bought the land is one of the wealthiest men in my home state today, a fact which is insignificant but tells me that Dad's instincts were right.

My mother, with her conservative, dogmatic "This is the way it's going to be" stance, ruled our home. That was the way I was raised, but the home JoBeth and I have made is different. Make no mistake—I have a strong, wonderful, wise, and loving wife. If you know her, you know that. If you don't know that, well, you don't know JoBeth. We do not always agree, but she has honored me by standing behind my decisions, good ones and bad.

I have been the pastor of five churches in our years together. Every time I have been called to another place of ministry, JoBeth has not wanted to leave. Not one single time. We would pray together, talk it over, but never has she wanted to leave a church I pastored and move to another place. And yet in every single instance she has said, "If you feel we should go, we'll go. I'll go wherever." Five times we have picked up our lives, left friends and familiar surroundings, and by faith moved out. You should know, too, that in every instance we went "backward" in terms of nickels and noses, from larger to smaller time after time. And she still said, "I'll go where you want me to go."

A parallel between the relationship of husband and wife and that of Jesus Christ and the church is drawn in Ephesians 5:24: "As the church is subject to Christ, so also the wives ought to be to their husbands." As the church relates to Christ in submission, so the wife is to relate to her husband in submission. This structure is the undergirding framework of the home, given because the One who made men and women knows how they function best. Some might argue that the writer of this particular message was a bachelor—and they would, in all probability, be correct. Perhaps we should give ear to a married man (the apostle Peter) as well:

> In the same way, you wives, be submissive to your own husbands so that even if any of them are disobedient to the word, they may be won without a word by the behavior of their wives. (1 Pet. 3:1)

SUBMISSION AS AN OPPORTUNITY

Unlike Paul, Peter had a wife. He lived most of his married life with his mother-in-law. Perhaps you think the influence of two women might temper his words on the topic of submission, but he echoes, through the inspiration of the Holy Spirit, the words of his unmarried brother, Paul. The wife is to be submissive to her own husband. But Peter goes further and says that there is an opportunity inherent in this choice.

If you are a Christian wife married to a man who is not a Christian, your submission in marriage can be more fruitful than you could ever imagine.

If you are a Christian wife married to a man who is not a Christian, your submission in marriage can be more fruitful than you could ever imagine. Peter says it can be a tool for God to use in drawing your husband to Him. I know a woman who has told me time and again, "My husband doesn't like you." Now you can't be everyone's best friend, but I thought I would ask why, just in case I had done something offensive that I wasn't aware of. She said she did not know why he felt that way, then went on: "For years when you'd come on television and my husband would leave the room, I'd wait until you got to a real good part of your sermon, then turn the volume up as loud as it would go, so that maybe he would hear. You never know, Pastor, he might just get saved through the walls." I don't blame him for hating me. Under those circumstances, I'd have to agree.

How does a Christian wife win her non-Christian husband? Without a word. You live your witness. And by your quiet, gentle, loving, submissive, prayerful, cooperative spirit, your husband may be touched. Maybe that's not your nature. That's fine. Decide now that, even though it might not come naturally, that is the wife you want to be and ask God to honor your intentions. You don't need to put tracts in his suitcase when he leaves town or have six deacons call him. You don't have to quote Scripture, sing hymns, or pray out loud for his shortcomings. (And I'd appreciate it if you'd keep the volume down to a reasonable decibel on us preacher types, too.) Just love him, love the Lord, and let him see the beauty of Christ in your life. You'll be amazed at its influence.

SUBMISSION AS AN ORNAMENT

Peter wins points in my book as an observant husband. As he lived with his wife he noticed the things that make a woman beautiful, and they were not all cosmetic.

> And let not your adornment be merely external—braiding the hair and wearing gold jewelry, or putting on dresses; but let it be the hidden person of the heart, with the imperishable quality of a gentle and quiet spirit, which is precious in the sight of God.
> (1 Pet. 3:3–4)

The word "adornment" here is the Greek word *cosmos,* from which the English word "cosmetics" is derived. I part company at this point with some who would say Peter is lobbying for "the natural look." This verse does not say "shun any external adornment, period." It does say, for goodness sake, don't stop there!

The key to real beauty goes beyond an attractive appearance. It is a matter of the heart.

In a church as large as ours, folks do all kinds of work, ordinary things and not-so-ordinary things. I know of several women in our congregation who are image consultants. I understand this is a booming industry with its own set of professional standards and many areas of specialization. One of these talented ladies who is a friend of my wife's tells me that it is next to impossible to make an unhappy woman—one who is dissatisfied, angry, or depressed—beautiful, no matter how lovely her features are. And even more surprising, she says that some of the most ordinary looking women imaginable by the world's standards possess a beauty that is utterly striking because of the condition of their hearts.

> *Some of the most ordinary looking women imaginable by the world's standards possess a beauty that is utterly striking because of the condition of their hearts.*

No cosmetic on the market today can adorn a woman like "a gentle and quiet spirit" can. A wife who chooses to submit to the leadership of her husband shines in a way that time can never dim. Her beauty is fool-proof—precious to God and to her mate. And better still, Peter doesn't say "take my word for it"; he illustrates his claim in the life of a well-known, flesh-and-blood woman:

> For in this way in former times the holy women also, who hoped in God, used to adorn themselves, being submissive to their own husbands. Thus Sarah obeyed Abraham, calling him lord, and you have become her children if you do what is right without being frightened by any fear. (1 Pet. 3:5-6)

The Most Beautiful Woman   Sarah, wife of the patriarch Abraham, had to be the most beautiful woman who ever lived. I believe she was magnificently beautiful—that she had an attractiveness about her that was uncommon and compelling. The pages of Genesis record the history of this amazing couple. At age 65 Sarah followed Abraham to Egypt, and fearing that Pharaoh would desire her for himself—and kill old Abraham to get him out of the way—he passed her off as his sister! Pharaoh did take her into his harem for a period of time, until Abraham confessed to Pharaoh that Sarah was truly his wife. For a 65-year-old woman to capture the attention of Pharaoh and cause her husband to fear the consequences of her beauty, she must have been a "10" by anyone's standard.

Then if that were not enough, when the two traveled on to the country of the Philistines, the Philistine king Abimilech set his sights on her as well. "Look," he said, "if she is your sister, I want her for my harem."

"No," Abraham said, "she's my wife."

Twenty-five years had gone by! Sarah by this time was 90 years old—and still obviously a desirable woman from a man's perspective. What made her so attractive? I am sure her "external adornment" was exceptional. But appearance changes with age, does it not? You do not see the "kings" of our day—men of power and wealth and status—with 90-year-old women on their arms, do you? In fact, it is usually just the opposite! What did Sarah have that drew men to her as if by magic?

Naturally, the Bible tells us, she was a jealous woman. By nature she was assertive, but functionally, in her relationship to her husband Abraham, she was submissive. They built a marriage that was more than a convenience, more than an "arrangement." It was a one-flesh union of love. When Sarah died at 127, Abraham could find no consolation. His grief was raw and real. He cried for days, weeks, months. He loved this woman, not for her physical beauty, but for "the imperishable quality of a gentle and quiet spirit." (1 Pet.

3:4). He loved her because she went with him through every change and challenge of life, even when he could not reasonably explain where it was that he was taking her.

Every enterprise has its leaders. Our nation has a president, congressmen, and senators. Every state in the nation has its governor and state representatives. Cities have mayors, councilmen, and city managers. These men and women are in positions of leadership over everyone else. Someone has to be in charge of the enterprise. But because I am not a president, senator, congressman, or mayor, does that mean I am inferior? Absolutely not. It simply means that being a president, senator, congressman, or mayor is not my job. It is not my function.

A woman in marriage is not inferior to a man. Any man that suggests that she is inferior is not worthy to be called a husband. Positionally, they are equal. Remember Galatians 3:28? Functionally, however, they are different.

Submission for the wife is an obligation, an opportunity, and an unfading ornament that enhances her beauty. It is to be offered by her "as to the Lord," not based on her assessment of her husband's proven ability or his performance as the leader of the home.

> *Submission for the wife is an obligation, an opportunity, and an unfading ornament that enhances her beauty in the eyes of her husband.*

Roles in marriage have changed. Expectations over the years for a man and wife have changed. Vows have even changed for some. But God's divine order for the home in marriage has never changed. His design is immutable and orderly, and in it there is great freedom and possibility. G. K. Chesterton's literary work was unified by the theme of the family, and in the early 1900s he perceived a "drift from domesticity" that alarmed him, yet appears tame in light of today's departure:

If Dick or Susan wish to destroy the family because they do not see the use of it, I say as I said in the beginning; if they do not see the use of it, they had much better preserve it. They have no business even to think of destroying it until they have seen the use of it.

The family mansion should be preserved or destroyed or rebuilt; it should not be allowed to fall to pieces brick by brick because nobody has any historic sense of the object of bricklaying. People do not know what they are doing; because they do not know what they are undoing.[1]

Marriage is an edifice built by God. In it, He assigned responsibilities to man and wife, understanding the nature of both. When people follow His design, the building is able to stand against almost anything. When they ignore it, the structure cannot support itself. He knew what He was doing. His design works.

QUESTIONS FOR FURTHER REFLECTION

1. Wife, is Jesus Christ your first priority? If He is, can you see submission to your husband as an act of reverence to Him? Do you agree to live in submission to your husband as the Bible instructs?

2. What (if any) attitudes of your own make submission difficult? What attitudes of others, including your husband, make submission a challenge?

3. Does the condition of your heart enhance your physical beauty? Wife, write a description of your heart as if you were looking at it in a mirror. Would you want the world to see it as you do? Why or why not?

4. Ask your husband what your willingness to follow his leadership means to him. His answer may surprise you!

5

A Strong
Word to
Husbands

I am convinced that fewer men would marry if they understood what marriage costs a man. Although single women are jokingly portrayed at times as over-eager for marriage, most single men that I have known have longed for the security of a home and a mate as much, or more, than women. Statistically, married men are healthier, happier, and tend to live longer than single men. Surveys have shown that married men are often more successful in terms of their career as well, out-earning single men on the average.

To a man marriage can look like the end to loneliness, one long, delightful date with his favorite girl, and the answer to his physical and domestic desires. If a man does think about the "costs" of marriage, he is most likely to do so in terms of finances. "Maybe," he reasons suspiciously, "two can't live as cheaply as one. And my taxes will increase. I'll have to keep her in clothes, we'll maintain two cars, not one. Then when children come, that will be other expenses."

He is wise, in whatever way, to count the costs. But finances are just the beginning of what marriage—at least marriage the way that God intended it—costs a man. The operative word in Scripture for a woman concerning marriage is submission. If women think that submission is a tough command to swallow, consider the awesome weight of the word that anchors the biblical message to husbands: sacrifice.

THE CALL TO SACRIFICIAL LOVE

"Which one of you," said Jesus, "when he wants to build a tower, does not first sit down and calculate the cost, to see if he has enough to complete it? Otherwise, when he has laid a foundation, and is not able to finish, all who observe it begin to ridicule him" (Luke 14:28-29). The cost of marriage to a man is sacrificial love. "Husbands," Paul wrote, "love your wives, just as Christ also loved the church and gave Himself up for her."(Eph. 5:25).

Sacrificial love is not giving-in love. That would be cheaper. It is giving-up love. Sacrificial love is not exemplified by the man who says, "Oh, I'd like to play golf today, but my wife wants to go shopping—so I'm going to go shopping with her." That's nice, certainly, but that's merely giving in.

> *Sacrifical love, giving-up love, is love that is willing to go to any lengths to provide for the well-being of the beloved.*

Sacrificial, giving-up love, is love that is willing to go to any lengths to provide for the well-being of the beloved. A man should count the cost before he marries, to determine whether or not he is willing to pay the price of being a real husband—but after he marries, he is to stop counting. Because whatever it takes to rightly love his wife is what he has promised to give, regardless of the cost.

Let me stop at this point and say that if a husband and wife both know and understand the biblical commands to each regarding marriage, but decide to obey only if or when their spouse "gets in line," they have missed the point entirely. The Bible says they are to be obedient to the Lord, period. Husbands, regardless of whether your wife obeys the biblical command of submission, you are to love sacrificially. Wives, even if your husband does not love you sacrificially, you are to submit to him as unto the Lord. Couples who are successfully married all agree that marriage is not a 50-50 proposition. Unless each partner intends to give 100 percent *regardless of a mate's performance*, a marriage is crippled from the start.

> *Marriage is not a 50-50 proposition. Unless each partner intends to give 100 percent regardless of a mate's performance, a marriage is crippled from the start.*

WHY SACRIFICIAL LOVE?

As a husband, I am to love my wife with a love that reminds her of Jesus Christ's love for her as a part of His church. I have been given an example to follow. Isn't it ironic that men who generally detest asking for or following a prescribed set of instructions are given a literal *picture*, a living diagram of what their love should resemble. Men, summon your courage and look at the picture of "fully assembled" married love you are to offer your wives.

Husbands, love your wives, just as Christ also loved the church *and gave Himself up for her.* (Eph. 5:25, emphasis added)

Christ loved the church in the purest, finest, most uncomplicated but complete way possible: He died for her. Paul explored this fact in Romans 5:6-8:

For while we were still helpless, at the right time Christ died for the ungodly. For one will hardly die for a righteous man; though perhaps for the good man someone would dare even to die. But God demonstrates His own love toward us, in that while we were yet sinners, Christ died for us.

A timeless hymn, *The Church's One Foundation* expresses this central, sacrificial truth using the imagery of marriage:

The church's one foundation
Is Jesus Christ her Lord;
She is his new creation
By Spirit and the Word:
From heaven he came and sought her,
To be his holy bride,
With his own blood he bought Her
And for her life he died.[1]

Jesus Christ gave his life for sinners, that we might be saved and know the one true God. He died so that we could live in Christ now and forever with Him in eternity. He loved the church so much He willingly gave His life for hers.

> *The problem with the Christian home is not that people have tried it and failed; the problem is they have not really put God's principles into operation.*

I believe 95 percent of the difficulty any woman might have with the principle of marital submission would disappear with daily exposure to a husband living sacrificially before her in the way that God commands. The problem with the Christian home is not that people have tried it and it has failed; the problem is they have not really put God's principles into operation. His way works—and when His precepts are practiced, every marriage succeeds.

THE HUSBAND AS LOVER AND LEADER

A husband who loves sacrificially will be the lover and leader in his own home. Far too many men today have abdicated the role of leadership and fallen short in the role of lover because they know that to lead and to love will mean sacrifice. Jesus gave Himself up for His church. He did not resign from His role as her leader; He used His own life to secure hers. What does it mean for a man to give up his life for his wife? It means that men are to open their lives fully to their wives. Goals, aspirations, fears, and joys are to be transparent before the loved one and her well-being is the first priority. Just as Jesus lived openly before His disciples, so husbands are to live with their wives.

Jesus lived sacrificially for the church and gave His life that she might be sanctified. Sanctification is a five-dollar preaching word, and one that hardly seems suited to a discussion of marriage, but Paul said Jesus gave Himself up for the church "that He might sanctify her, having cleansed her by the washing of water with the word, that He might present to Himself the church in all her glory, having no spot or wrinkle or any such thing; but that she should be holy and blameless"(Eph. 5:26-27). A husband is to present his wife to the world in the same way.

A Love That Sanctifies

> *A woman who is genuinely loved by her husband has a spark, a confident smile, a spontaneity about her that is nothing less than beautiful.*

The most intimate spiritual relationship I know is the relationship between Jesus Christ and the church. The most intimate social relationship I know is the relationship between a husband and a wife. I do not imagine the church was anything close to spotless before Christ loved her with a sacrificial love. But His love *sanctified* her, making what was flawed by nature perfect in redemption.

I have not met a man yet who would say he married a perfect wife. All are sinners, and all have flaws. But I have noticed that about a woman who is genuinely loved by her husband has a spark, a confident smile, a spontaneity about her that is nothing less than beautiful. And while I do not profess to be a prophet, I believe

I could spend just a short time talking with any wife and know whether or not she is really loved by her husband. Sacrificial love has a sanctifying element about it that is reflected in the radiance of the beloved.

Why don't men love this way instinctively? If "boys will be boys," as the saying goes, why won't men be men? Some men marry and slowly begin to think of their wives as they would a mother: someone to satisfy their physical needs, feed them, clothe them, and protect their delicate and sensitive egos. However, this is not the biblical view of married love. Others marry then virtually ignore the woman they chose to be their wife, failing to nurture the relationship past the altar "I do's."

Did you know that the *average* couple spends 37 minutes a week in conversation? Thirty-seven minutes a week. Is it any wonder, then, that when the children grow up and leave the nest, divorce often follows? After all, these two people have only talked 37 minutes a week all these years—they hardly know one another except as joint custodians of a household and children!

Oh, but the husband who loves his wife sacrificially *sanctifies* her by living in such a way that he would give his life for her. As one writer has said,

> Holy matrimony, like other holy orders, was never intended as a comfort station for lazy people. On the contrary, it is a systematic program of deliberate and thoroughgoing self-sacrifice. A man's home is not his castle so much as his monastery, and if he happens to be treated like a king there, then it is only so that he might be better enabled to become a servant."[2]

Love your wife with a sanctifying love.

A Love That   The apostle Paul wrote:
Satisfies

> So husbands ought also to love their own wives as their own bodies. He who loves his own wife loves himself;

for no one ever hated his own flesh, but nourishes and cherishes it, just as Christ also does the church. (Eph. 5:28-29)

A man who loves his wife sacrificially loves her in a satisfying way. If husband and wife are "one flesh" in marriage, to hurt her is to hurt himself, and to do good to her is do himself good. Husbands are to know what is satisfying to their wives—what things bring them joy and pleasure—and seek to give those things. Do you know those things? Do I?

To determine whether or not I knew the things that were satisfying to my wife, I gave myself a little test. Let me encourage you to try it too. Take a piece of paper, and on it write down the three things your wife most enjoys. Then give it to her, and ask her how you did. I have to confess that the first time I tried this, I was one for three. It is amazing how insensitive men can be. No woman—or very few—could live with a man long and not know *at least* three things that were satisfying to him. Women pick up with ease what most men wouldn't get in a six-hour crash course. But far too many men could not write down three things their wives most enjoy.

> *Imagine how many marriages would improve if a man attempted to know his wife as well as he knew his own body and to treat her with as much care as his own flesh.*

Paul understood this gender difference and encouraged men to love their wives as they loved their own bodies, in a way that is satisfying and on-target. Men know their own bodies. They know about how much they weigh and how many cups of coffee will keep them from falling asleep. They know how many miles they can jog before their knees begin to ache, and whether a nagging pain can be ignored or needs a doctor's attention. They listen to their bodies.

Imagine how many marriages would improve if a man attempted to know his wife as well as he knew his own body and to treat her with as much care and respect as he did his own flesh. To do that, men would have to make a careful study of their mates. Do you know what makes your wife smile? Laugh out loud? Do you know what she can do for hours without getting bored? What makes her cry? What music she unconsciously hums? What she considers her favorite way to spend a day?

If men are to love their wives with a satisfying love, they will learn these things. Begin where you are to study your wife and pay close attention to what makes her unique. Your marriage will be richer for the effort.

A Love That Sympathizes   Another facet of sacrificial love is *sympathy*. This word is relegated to hushed tones and unctious greeting cards—but at its heart, sympathy is understanding. The married apostle Peter, perhaps from the breadth of his domestic experience, urged husbands to live "sympathetically" with their wives:

> You husbands, likewise, live with your wives in an understanding way, as with a weaker vessel, since she is a woman. (1 Pet. 3:7)

Someone once asked Dr. Albert Einstein's wife if she understood the theory of relativity. "No," she responded, "but I understand the doctor." Men, you may not understand womankind, but you'd better do your best to understand the kind of woman you married.

Understand that because she is a woman, your mate responds differently than you do, and never cease to take that fact into account. A few years ago, Gary Smalley and John Trent led a "Love Is a Decision" seminar in our church. They illustrated the differences in the sexes by equating a man with a buffalo and a woman with a butterfly. Buffalos are large, sturdy, rugged beasts; they're not bothered by much. A butterfly, on the other hand, is delicate, tiny, sensitive.

The average woman speaks twice as many words daily as the average man. Women tend to be more relational. They find a football game, for instance, is more interesting if they know something about the players on either team. Men tend to be more goal oriented; "recreational shopping" is a contradiction in terms to most men. When a man shops, nine times out of ten he goes straight for the item he is after—and then he goes home. (Understand that I am talking in generalities here—and strictly for the purpose of illustrating some built-in differences, not to say one way is preferable to another.)

As a man charged to sacrificially love my wife, I need to understand her way of relating and respect her sensitive nature. I need to love her with a sympathetic love that says I understand her feelings and care about her struggles. Although nearly as many women work outside the home as do not, men still dominate the work force in sheer numbers. And men tend to get their needs for recognition, achievement, and admiration met in the workplace. Their ego is fed outside the home. Even working women, however, desire to get positive feedback from the people they are closest to—their families. A man's identity is forged more by his work than his relationships; and the opposite usually holds true for women.

> *As a man charged to sacrifically love my wife, I need to understand her way of relating and respect her sensitive nature.*

For the modern woman, this presents a kind of double-bind. If she is a member of the workforce, she is involved in an uphill climb. Women are still compensated less than men, and "the glass ceiling" keeps many talented women from attaining positions of power and influence. And if she chooses to stay at home, her support system is nowhere near as well-structured as it might have been decades ago when the majority of other wives did so.

The average American today moves once every four years. Such frequent moves don't allow for the building of deep relationships in most cases. While extended families living together under the same roof were once common, now it is rare that a woman would have her mother, sister, or aunt living with her. A hundred years ago, a young wife who was pregnant would have relatives with her throughout her pregnancy, and they would be there to give assistance when the baby was born, teaching the new mother to care for her child. A hundred years ago, women canned together, sewed together, went to church together. An intimacy—a comraderie—developed in the doing of ordinary things together day in and day out. A support system existed for women in a way that it does not today.

Before someone decides I want go back to pioneer ways, let me explain. My point is simply this: Men today need to be more sensitive than ever to the needs of their wives for fellowship, support, intellectual and spiritual growth, and emotional nurture. If they are to live with their wives in an understanding way, they need some inkling of how demanding a woman's life can be! Gentlemen, when your wife goes to aerobics class or to a Bible study group or to a club or activity, understand her need. Do not say "Why do you do all that stuff? Why do you go all the time when I'm at home?" Accept responsibility, especially if you have small children, and say instead, "Hey, this is your day. I've got the kids. You go, and I'll enjoy being with them." The amazing thing is—you just might!

A Love That Supremely Honors

Sacrificial love bestows honor on the beloved. "Grant her honor," the apostle Peter said of husbands to wives, "as a fellow heir of the grace of life" (1 Pet. 4:7). A husband is to love his wife sympathetically as a "weaker vessel," understanding their differences, but he is to love her supremely as the magnificent creation and gift of God that she is. I have never understood men who belittle their wives or vice versa. To cut down the woman he marries—in public or in private—is to cast doubt on his own intelligence and decision-making ability. Whether in terms of appearance or personality, the man who verbally diminishes his wife makes an enormous mistake.

To honor something is to ascribe value to it. Priority is given to things but people are honored. The president of the United States is honored by the playing of "Hail to the Chief," and by hundreds of other acts of protocol, large and small. Men, would your wives know by your actions that you honor them? Could they tell by the things you say and do that you value them above anyone else? Gary Smalley describes honor as "a reflex of the heart toward one who is deeply treasured." I like that definition. Honor is the overflow of a loving heart.

Ask your wife what would honor her. You might be surprised at how simple it would be to bestow this gift of sacrificial love. Maybe it is a phone call to say you are running late. Or an offer to drop dry cleaning off on your way to work. Or a warm hug at the end of a day that's been as demanding for her as it has for you. Or even the simple words "I love you," spoken at just the right time.

When a man dates his future wife, he does whatever it takes to win her and to convince her that she is the center of his world. In a letter to his fiance Frances, G. K. Chesterton honored her with these words that would almost certainly strike a chord in the heart of any woman:

> There are four lamps of thanksgiving always before him. The first is for his creation out of the same earth with such a woman as you. The second is that he has not, with all his faults, "gone after strange women." You cannot think how a man's self-restraint is rewarded

in this. The third is that he has tried to love everything alive: a dim preparation for loving you. And the fourth is—but no words can express that. Here ends my previous existence. Take it: it led me to you.[3]

In the first blush of courtship men are right there with what their loved one needs. They are Mr. Courteous, Mr. Suave, Mr. Nice, Mr. Thoughtful. But as the years go by how insensitive they become. Sacrificial love loves its object supremely—before all others and before all else. It cannot do anything less.

How are husbands to love their wives? They are to love them with a sacrificial love. They are to love them with a love that sanctifies. They are to love them with a love that satisfies. They are to love them with a love that sympathizes. And they are to love them with a love that is supreme—superior to all other earthly loves. Why are they to do this? Let's look at the last phrase in 1 Peter 3:7: "so that your prayers may not be hindered." If husbands are not loving their wives in the way God commands, their prayers are hindered.

If there is something wrong in a husband's relationship with his wife, he as the lover and leader of the home is at fault. A husband should be the one to lead out in forgiveness, to communicate, to offer sympathy, and to live sacrificially before his wife. I wonder how the apostle learned this? What circumstances did the Holy Spirit use to teach this husband that his marriage relationship affected his prayer life?

> *A husband should be the one to lead out in forgiveness, to communicate, to offer sympathy, and to live sacrifically before his wife.*

Imagine Peter out preaching all day in the streets, dodging criticism, and the demands of the fledgling church from morning until night. Then he goes home to his wife and her family—we know that he lived with his mother-in-law for some time—relieved to be out of the whirlwind of another trying day. "I'm home," he calls. "What's for supper?"

He crosses the room to the stove, picks up the lid on a simmering pot, turns up his nose, and says, "Oh, no. Not fish again. We just had fish." Mrs. Peter begins to cry. She's had a tough day with the kids, the roof is leaking, and her mother has been difficult to deal with. She flings off her apron, still in tears, and rushes to the other room. He is dumbfounded. "What did I say? All I wanted to know was what we are having for supper. I like fish. Fish is fine. What did I do, for goodness sake?"

He follows her to their bedroom, and through the door she calls out, "Go away. I don't want to talk to you!"

He exits through the back door, giving it a good slam, and paces out in the yard. "I don't understand women," he says. "I sure don't understand my wife. I've been out all day. Everyone's been against me. I've preached. I've performed miracles. I'm an apostle. I knew Jesus Christ. I cannot understand what in the world is the matter with that woman." He thinks for a minute, then says to himself *I think I'll just pray for a while and see if I can get things straightened out.* So Peter prays under a fig tree there in the yard. Nothing. It's as if the heavens are brass. "Lord, I'm praying in Jesus' name," he says. Still nothing.

So he walks around a little more. "I don't understand this." Then a light comes on. "I wonder if she's had a tough day too? I wonder if there's something else bothering her that I haven't thought to ask about?" He stops pacing. "Maybe my first question shouldn't have been about dinner. How stupid of me! How insensitive to just barge through the door bellowing, What's for dinner?' I never said a kind word, never kissed her, never gave her a hug. What a dumb, stupid lout I am."

Then he notices that a rose bush is blooming nearby. He walks over, picks a few, and removes the thorns.

Quietly he carries them inside, goes back to the closed door of their room, and walks in. Without saying a word he goes to her, kneels before her, and places the flowers gently in her lap. "Oh, Pete," she says. "You shouldn't have."

"You know me," he begins. "I talk too much. I'm always putting my foot in my mouth—speaking before I've had a chance to think. I'm sorry. Fish will be great. I love fish—used to think a man couldn't have too many. Most of all I love you. Tell me about your day, and let's start over."

The two of them talk a little bit, then very naturally kneel down to pray together in that little room which was dark just moments before, but now is bathed in warm light. God is present. His glory is there in their love and sharing and tears and reconciliation. Their prayers are heard—and there is a joy and intimacy that was missing earlier.

I am not ready for God to deal with me in prayer until I have been obedient to Him—and that obedience extends to the way I honor my wife as my fellow heir of grace. As a husband, an unhindered relationship with my wife is critical to my prayer life! Husbands, love your wives as Christ loved the church and gave Himself up for her. The operative word for husbands is *sacrifice.*

A prominent Christian speaker and author once received a letter from a woman who moved with her new husband to a small apartment. After they had lived in this place for a short while, they noticed a noise in the ceiling and soon discovered that a mouse was living there as well.

This woman could tolerate a lot of things, but mice were not on the list. So her energetic new husband went to work, setting out traps, baiting them, and waiting for the inevitable. Sure enough, in a day or two, they caught the unwanted "roommate," but the mousetrap did not kill him. Now they had a problem, since they didn't want to just kill him "in cold blood." Her letter then went on to describe how they placed the mouse, trap and all, in a bucket of water, thinking that the most compassionate way to dispose of him would be to drown him.

Not wanting to watch him struggle, they put the bucket out of the way and left the house for a while. When they returned, they were shocked to see that the mouse was still struggling for all he was worth, propped up on the trap, to keep his tiny nose just a fraction of an inch above the water line.

Her letter did not say what happened to the mouse—but her story provided a graphic illustration for the real reason she wrote. "My marriage," she said, "has been like that mouse for years—standing on one aching toe with its nose just barely out of the water."

> *God has ordained responsibilities for the man and woman in marriage, and as they follow His percepts, they begin to see marriage as it was meant to be.*

I wonder how many marriages are like that today. Maybe other people look at you and your mate with envy—but you know the real story. Perhaps other friends or co-workers come to you for help with their own marital problems, not knowing how deeply you struggle in your own union. God's way works. God has ordained responsibilities for the man and woman in marriage, and as they follow his precepts, they begin to see marriage as it was meant to be.

Writing from his Tegel prison cell in 1943, Dietrich Bonhoeffer outlined those responsibilities in a sermon for two friends marrying in his absence:

> You may order your home as you like, except in one thing: the wife is to be subject to her husband, and the husband is to love his wife. In this way God gives to husband and wife the honour that is due to each. The wife's honour is to serve the husband, to be a "help

meet for him," as the creation story has it; and the husband's honour is to love his wife with all his heart.[4]

If you are a husband, the responsibility begins with you. Love your wife with a sacrificial love. A marriage has no better foundation than this.

QUESTIONS FOR FURTHER REFLECTION

1. Husband, describe sacrificial love as you understand it. Ask your wife what that kind of love means to her.
2. Do you agree with the following statement? And why or why not? "I believe 95 percent of the difficulty any woman might have with the principle of marital submission would disappear with daily exposure to a husband living sacrificially before her in the way that God commands."
3. Husband, could you truthfully say you know your wife as well as you know your own body? Does your wife feel that you love her as you love yourself? (If you're not sure, ask her!)
4. Ask your wife what words or actions would prove to her that you honor her. Strive to express your honor for her in ways that she values.

PART THREE

FANNING
THE FLAMES

6

WHY HUG?

A Wife Needs:
Affection

PSYCHOTHERAPIST AND MARRIAGE
and family therapist Dr. Willard Harley, in his excellent
book, *His Needs Her Needs*, outlines the top five needs
in marriage for husbands and wives. Based on observations gleaned from thousands of couples he has coun-
seled in his career, Dr. Harley identifies these needs:

The Top 5 Needs of a Wife
1. Affection
2. Conversation
3. Honesty and Openness
4. Financial Support
5. Family Commitment

The Top 5 Needs of a Husband
1. Sexual Fulfillment
2. Recreational Companionship
3. Attractive Spouse

4. Domestic Support
5. Admiration[1]

What struck me immediately about these lists, which I believe to be fairly accurate, is the fact that absolutely no overlap exists between the two. A man and woman meet, fall in love, and marry with the hopes that their needs will be met. They each give what they long to receive, then become confused when it does not seem to satisfy their spouse. Some might take issue with the order of the lists, or insist that all the items do not apply in their case—and they will not, for everyone. But for argument's sake, let us agree that *generally* these needs are felt by most husbands and most wives.

If so, the number one need of a woman in marriage is affection. Affection is the optimum "room temperature" of a happy marriage. Imagine your marriage as an empty room. Using your thermostat, you adjust the temperature of the room to keep it at its most comfortable, regardless of the weather outside. For some, optimum room temperature is 68 degrees. For others, 72 degrees seems ideal. But whatever "room temperature" is in your home, in your marriage, the optimum "room temperature" is affection. Affection should be the underlying atmosphere of marriage twenty-four hours a day, seven days a week.

> *Affection should be the underlying atmosphere of marriage twenty-four hours a day, seven days a week.*

C. S. Lewis saw it not only as a kind of love, but as one that permeates all the other "greater loves," much to their good. "Affection," he wrote, "besides being a love itself, can enter into the other loves and colour them all through and become the very medium in which they operate from day to day. They would not perhaps wear very well without it."[2]

If men could understand that simple concept, it would radically change their marriages—and they need to understand it not just rationally, but in practice. A woman's need for affection is so strong that the unfulfilled desire for it can lead to an extramarital affair. Most professional counselors agree that women are unfaithful for completely different reasons from men. While lust can cause many a man to stray, a woman can literally be hugged into an affair if her marriage is void of affection.

Let me say two things parenthetically in this regard. First, it is never right to have an affair. It is never right to be unfaithful to your mate, but people are, and we need to understand why. Second, there is nothing wrong with hugging between family and friends. It is an accepted part of our culture. If someone colors a hug between friends with some sort of sexual overtones, that person has a problem.

Having said those two things, let us take a look at this affection that most women desire. The simplest, most readily mastered expression of affection is a hug. Its benefits are manifold:

> *While lust can cause many a man to stray, a woman can literally be hugged into an affair if her marriage is void of affection.*

> It's the perfect cure for what ails you. No movable parts; no batteries to wear out; no periodic check ups; low energy consumption; high energy yield; inflation-proof; non-taxable; non-polluting; and, of course, fully returnable. Hugging is healthy. It relieves tension, combats depression, reduces stress, and improves blood circulation. It's invigorating, it's rejuvenating, it elevates self-esteem, it generates good will, it has no unpleasant side effects. It is nothing less than a miracle drug.[3]

Inspirational speaker Zig Ziglar calls his wife Jean "the Happy Hugger," and says that regardless of the hour, when he comes home he is *always* greeted with a big hug. He is quick to note, too, that no one feels like hugging all the time, but a caring husband will make the effort, even when he doesn't feel like it, knowing that there will be few times when his wife will not appreciate that small demonstration of his affection.

LET'S TALK   Men and women are different. If you think it is silly to state the obvious, think again. Both men and women *need* the reminder that they have married a foreigner. I like the title of a hot seller I saw recently in the bookstore that hammers that fact home: *Men Are from Mars, Women Are from Venus.* It does seem that way at times.

Talk is another expression of affection for a woman, and the love of it begins early. A few years ago I was visiting with my granddaughter, Lee Beth. We played a while, then we ran a while—we *did* things together. That was my way, I guess, of showing her affection: doing things together. She obviously enjoyed herself, too, but before long she had another idea. "Goosie," (that's me) she said, "let's go back in my room. I want to tell you something." So we went to her little room, she closed the door, we climbed up on the bed, and she said, "I have some secrets to tell you." She began to tell me some little things, and I listened, and then she said, "Now you tell me some secrets."

Now I had three boys, and not a one of them ever told me a secret or asked me to tell them one. But this is the way little girls play. They deepen relationships with talk and the sharing of special secrets. So I managed to think of a few secrets to tell her, too, and she was thrilled. Women even at four like to communicate. They cultivate intimacy that way.

It is not the same with men, big or little. They play ball, or watch it when their playing days are over. They build forts and chase bad guys, or watch action movies. They golf. They fish. And even if they do not say much to one another, through their activities they become better friends.

Applying this truth to marriage means that a part of showing wives affection is communicating with them—talking, and really listening. How many men have suddenly heard their wife say, "Did you hear what I said?" or "Are you listening?" I am often guilty here. When my middle son Ben was just a boy, he would tell me something on occasion and suspect that he did not have my undivided attention. At those times he would crawl up into my lap, take my face in both of his hands, hold it close to his, and say, "Daddy, I'm telling you something." He was. And there were times that I was not really listening like I should have been.

This has happened more than once, too, when JoBeth and I travel. She would say, "Would you like to stop here and get something to drink?"

"No," I would answer, "no, I'm fine."

We would press on for a while, and eventually she would say, "You know, I'm thirsty. I wish you had stopped back there."

And I would respond, "Why didn't you tell me you were thirsty? We would have stopped."

"I asked *you* if *you* were thirsty," she always said. "I thought you'd ask me if I was thirsty." Men can be so slow. A man thinks everyone including his wife should be straightforward, up front. A woman thinks everyone including her husband should solicitously build a concensus that would please all parties.

But men and women do not respond in like manner—and never will. By his attentiveness to his wife and his desire to communicate with her in a meaningful way, a man demonstrates affection.

I can already hear some put-out husband complaining: "It's just not my nature to be affectionate. My wife knew when she married me I was not the affectionate type."

AFFECTION, PERIOD

But I will bet you *were* the "affectionate type" when you courted her, or she would not have married you! If you want your marriage to sizzle, work at being that type again. I understand it is tough. You do not want to pretend to be something you are not, or to act in a way that is phony. Maybe you feel silly writing notes or sending flowers, and you think it is ridiculous to call your wife during the day if you do not have anything significant to say—but you do! Just your call says "I love you" to your wife and tells her that you are glad she is yours.

Men do things every day that are "not our nature." It is not my nature to sit in meetings for several hours, but there are times that I do so. It is not my nature to be sweet and affectionate, either, but with practice I can make it a habit. I remember walking through the den one day and seeing JoBeth scratch our dog Sonny's back. She rubbed Sonny's back and he was just so content that I said, "You know, I wish you'd rub my back like that." She didn't miss a beat. She said, "If you were as sweet as Sonny, I would!" So I'm working on it.

> *There's not a woman alive who doesn't know the difference between affection, period, and affection, comma.*

While I was preaching the series of sermons on marriage that form the basis of this book, I decided I'd better be sure I was practicing at home what I proclaimed from the pulpit. I took JoBeth out to dinner, and I had flowers delivered to her at our table! She was so pleased. Then I took her to the high school basketball game. And if that's not the perfect crowning touch to a romantic dinner for two, I don't know what is! The whole point is that we men need to work at showing affection.

One more little secret on the art of showing affection: you should have no ulterior motive. There is not a woman alive who does not know the difference between affection, period, and affection, comma. The affection that satisfies your wife's desire has no strings attached. A hug is a hug, not a prelude to sex or the announcement that you have just bought a boat. The husband who seldom touches his wife except as an entree to lovemaking needs to understand that he is depriving her of something as important to her as sex is to him: the knowledge that she is loved and appreciated, period.

"There is indeed," C. S. Lewis wrote, "a peculiar charm, both in friendship and in Eros, about those moments when Appreciative love lies, as it were, curled up asleep, and the mere ease and ordinariness of the relationship (free as solitude, yet neither is alone) wraps us round. No need to talk. No need to make love. No needs at all except perhaps to stir the fire."[4] Moments like these are the bread and butter of marriage.

I wonder sometimes what the wedding party, guests, and pastor would hear at the marriage altar if the bride and groom's thoughts were broadcast. I imagine an eager groom thinking, *Boy, I've got a gal here who will meet all of my needs. I've had a poor self-image all my life, but now I have someone who really loves me and I am thrilled to be with her!*

A breathless bride stands beside him, and her thoughts race with his: *I'm so glad I've found this guy who will meet all of the needs of my life. When we are married all of my troubles with family, friends, relationships, and work will just melt away!*

This is what I call a "tick on the dog" relationship. A tick is a parasite in the insect world. It sees a host, attaches itself to that host, and has itself a nourishing meal. But when a husband and wife *both* look at the other person as their "meal ticket" to lifelong satisfaction, what you have is two ticks and no dog, or to put it in a more current vernacular, two takers and no givers. It is not hard to see trouble ahead for a relationship of this sort.

SECURITY AND SIGNIFICANCE

Needs are not wrong. Every human being has two basic needs: the need for security and the need for significance. These are, at their root, spiritual needs, but they manifest themselves in the natural aspects of life. The need for security is manifested in a man or woman's desire to be unconditionally, totally loved, to be accepted regardless of their appearance or performance. All long for that kind of security.

The need for significance is evident in the desire people have for their lives to count for something: to produce or nurture or leave behind things of real, lasting value. The trouble with coming to marriage expecting these deep needs to be met *by a spouse* is that no one can do so! Wives, you have married a sinner. Wonderful as he may be, he cannot provide you with permanent security and significance. Husbands, you have married a sinner. No matter how gracious and kind and supportive she is, she cannot supply you with the lasting security and significance you long for.

> *Marriage does not make you whole. Jesus Christ makes you whole. He and He alone is the solution to man's needs for security and significance.*

I tell the thousands of single adults in our church fellowship every chance I get that marriage is not the solution to anyone's problems, nor can it fulfill all of their desires. If you are unhappy and unfulfilled single, count on more of the same as a married person. Marriage does not make you whole. Jesus Christ makes you whole. He and He alone is the solution to man's needs for security and significance. Look at what the Bible has to say about the security God provides:

> I give eternal life to them, and they shall never perish; and no one shall snatch them out of My hand. My Father, who has given them to me, is greater than all; and no one is able to snatch them out of the Father's hand. (John 10:28-29)

I have loved you with an everlasting love; therefore I have drawn you with loving kindness. (Jer. 31:3)

For I am convinced that neither death, nor life, nor angels, nor principalities, nor things present, nor things to come, nor powers, nor height, nor depth, nor any other created thing, shall be able to separate us from the love of God, which is in Christ Jesus our Lord. (Rom. 8:38-39)

And about the significance He bestows:

Yet Thou hast made him a little lower than God, and dost crown him with glory and majesty! Thou dost make him to rule over the works of Thy hands; Thou hast put all things under his feet. (Ps. 8:5-6)

The Spirit Himself bears witness with our spirit that we are children of God, and if children, heirs also, heirs of God and fellow heirs with Christ, if indeed we suffer with Him in order that we may also be glorified with Him. (Rom. 8:16-17)

Then God said, "Let Us make man in Our image, according to Our likeness; and let them rule over the fish of the sea and over the birds of the sky and over cattle and over all the earth, and over every creeping thing that creeps on the earth." And God created man in His own image, in the image of God He created him, male and female He created them. . . And God saw all that He had made, and behold, it was very good. (Gen. 1:26-28, 31)

Dr. Robert McGee is founder and president of Rapha, a national provider of in-hospital, Christ centered psychiatric and substance abuse counseling. In his book *Search for Significance*, Dr. McGee relates that every believer is "deeply loved by God, completely forgiven, full pleasing, totally accepted, and complete in Christ,"[5] and that this knowledge results in a life of love and depth and meaning.

Understanding that your deepest needs for security and significance can only be met by God in Christ frees you to give your spouse the things you *can* offer, and that includes affection. When Jesus Christ meets these needs, the security and significance imparted by an affectionate spouse become a grace gift.

HOW DO WE LEARN AFFECTION? Some of you men may be thinking you are at a loss when it comes to showing the woman you married affection. Maybe you are not sure what really satisfies her desire in this area. I have a revolutionary suggestion: ask her! You are married to the best teacher in the world. Wives are "Phi Beta Kappa" in affection. They know what to do. JoBeth writes little notes for me when I travel. She is thoughtful about this, interested in that, and on and on. She knows how to express affection. And if I ask her, she can readily describe the kind of affection she'd like to receive from me. When men do that, the mystery is solved. They are without excuse.

The Bible even gives us a starting place for the work of demonstrating affection in Ephesians 4:32: "And be kind to one another," Paul writes, "tender-hearted, forgiving each other, just as God in Christ has also forgiven you." My good friend Cliff Barrows says that there are 12 words that can breathe life into any relationship: *I am sorry. I was wrong. Please forgive me. I love you.* These are words of tenderhearted kindness and affection, and the one who remembers and uses them will soon come to understand their power to change the hardest of hearts and the most hopeless of circumstances.

A woman who had not been feeling well was taken to see a physician by her husband, who was becoming concerned about her condition. "This woman is perfectly all right," the doctor declared. "There is nothing physically wrong with her." The husband, who had observed her listlessness for some time, was not so easily convinced. "I don't know, Doc. She seems so down and depressed. Couldn't you recommend some kind of treatment?" The doctor thought for a moment. "I'll tell you what she needs," he said. And he stood, crossed over to the wife, hugged her, and kissed her. "She needs that three times a week," he told the husband. "Well," her husband countered, "I can bring her up here on Tuesday and Thursday, but I play golf on Saturday."

What is the point? The affection your wife needs must come from you. No one else can provide this the way you can. And no one else is commanded to.

The affection your wife needs must come from you. No one else can provide this the way you can. And no one else is commanded to.

Do not forget, gentlemen, that the love you have for your wives should resemble the love of Jesus Christ for the church. When it does, your marriage, in its everyday, ordinary functioning, preaches a sermon to non-believers. Would a non-Christian be interested in the love of Christ by observing the intricacies of your marriage?

Ruth Bell Graham, wife of evangelist Billy Graham, had been at home alone for several weeks while Billy was traveling on a crusade. The Grahams had four children then, all of whom Ruth says were poor sleepers. She found herself up half a dozen times each night with one or another of the children, as tired in the morning as she was when she fell into bed the night before.

One particular morning at breakfast, she picked baby Franklin up out of his crib and set him in his high chair before changing his diaper. Ruth, with no makeup and unbrushed hair, presided over the morning bedlam of three other children at the breakfast table. Every time her older daughter Gigi would begin to talk, Bunny, the younger one, would interrupt. Finally Gigi threw her fork into the middle of the table and announced "Mother, between looking at you, smelling Franklin, and listening to Bunny, I've lost my appetite."

Sometimes it is little wonder that wives lose their appetite for physical love. And even less a wonder that those who may not know Him lose their appetite for the Lord when they observe us. Why hug? Because it costs so little and it can do so much! Hug your wife every chance you get . . . then wait for her to return the favor. You will not be sorry you did!

QUESTIONS FOR FURTHER REFLECTION

1. Write down the top five ways you are likely to express affection. Have your mate do likewise and exchange lists. Are your ways of expressing affection similar or different? How do any differences that exist affect your relationship?

2. Does your expression of affection ever carry ulterior motives? How likely are you to hug your mate for "no reason?"

3. Often unmet needs for security or significance undermine a marriage. Discuss any unmet needs in these areas with your mate, understanding that he or she will never be able to completely satisfy them. Only Jesus can do that.

7

"Tired in Lincoln, Nebraska"

A Husband Needs:
Sexual Fulfillmemt

SHE WROTE, EVIDENTLY, TO GET THE thing off her chest once and for all. "Tired in Lincoln, Nebraska," had a sex problem—and she took it to Abigail Van Buren, "Dear Abby" to millions of Americans. This is what she had to say:

> Dear Abby: At age 50, after 30 years of marriage, I would like to forget about sex altogether. Believe me, I've paid my dues. I suspect that many, if not most, women get very little physical satisfaction out of sex: they just go through the motions because they want to do something for the men they love. Please poll your readers, and if they are honest, I think you'll find I am right. Tired in Lincoln, Nebraska.[1]

Abby did poll her readers. And when the "votes" were in, some 250,000 women had written, most agreeing with "Tired" that they would willingly give up the act of sex in return for a little affection from their husbands. Syndicated columnist Jim Sanderson wrote a follow-up on these amazing—to husbands, anyway—results:

> To date nearly a quarter of a million women have written in and more than 50 percent agreed with "Tired." Absolutely astounding. Totally depressing. You thought it was the sexual revolution that was raising the divorce rate. It's the un-sexual revolution. Can you imagine 30 years with a woman who was only going through the motions? How about 20 years? Ten years? If "Tired" still loves her husband after 30 years, he is not an animal. He is a human being who has responded to his wife's needs in many ways.
>
> You cannot believe the frustration and ultimately the anger a man feels, in trying to excite and express his love to a woman who, month after month, year after year, is only paying her dues. Quite often her passive resistance finally defeats him. He forgets the joy and strength he once knew. She emasculates him.
>
> It's not just middle-aged women, either. The tragedy of our sexual revolution is both that it has over-whelmed some people and not touched others at all. Our society is interlaced with tired females of all ages, passive women who, in a kind of smug, stubborn pride, won't take charge, even of their own bodies, much less their lives. Their glory is to suffer nobly.
>
> It's women who insist endlessly that they cannot have sex without love. But how can a married woman have love without sex? Is it physically possible? Doesn't she see that sex is the very apex of love's pyramid—the final stage you move to when your words and gestures do not suffice to express the depths of your feeling?

Sex in marriage is love. The physical union, not only of two bodies, but two souls. Marital love is debased when it only comes to mean nothing but affection, shared experience and kind words.[2]

If the greatest need of a wife in marriage is affection, the intense desire is matched in men by the need for sexual fulfillment. "Tired in Lincoln, Nebraska," apparently could not understand that need of her husband, even after 30 years of marriage. Evidently many other women share her "take-it-or-leave-it" attitude. "Tired" wanted to forego sex in exchange for affection, but both are integral to a satisfying marriage.

> *If the greatest need of a wife in marriage is affection, the intense desire is matched in men by the need for sexual fulfillment.*

If affection is the atmosphere of a healthy marriage, sex is an event that takes place within that atmosphere. And as husbands are responsible for providing the atmosphere of affection, wives are obligated to meet their husbands need for sexual fulfillment. The apostle Paul writes:

> Let the husband fulfill his duty to the wife, and likewise also the wife to her husband. The wife does not have authority over her own body, but the husband does; and likewise also the husband does not have authority over his own body, but the wife does. Stop depriving one another, except by agreement for a time that you may devote yourselves to prayer, and come together again lest Satan tempt you because of your lack of self-control. (1 Cor. 7:3-5)

Ladies, out of the millions and millions of people in this world, your husband selected you, under God, to be his wife. One of the greatest needs of the man that you married is sexual fulfillment, and by marrying you, he agreed that you are the one woman he desires and trusts to satisfy this need. Other people can serve him coffee. Other people can keep his calendar, answer his mail, and schedule his day. Others can even keep his clothes clean, pick up after him, entertain and support him—but in God's plan, only you, his wife, can meet this, his most felt need.

A wife might say, "I provide delicious, healthy meals for my husband every day of his life." Your husband can go to a restaurant and be well-fed. Or she might reason, "I wash his clothes." Your husband can drop his clothes off at the laundry and pick them up that same day. "I am his friend," she might offer. "I listen to him." I applaud that, but your husband has friends in other places, even if they are not as loyal or ready to listen as you. But there is one thing under God that no one else can do for him, and that is meet his physical, sexual needs. That opportunity and responsibility is yours and yours alone.

Sex Saturation

Is there not enough already written on sex to preclude a chapter on it in a "religious" book? Should I not stick to the high ground in this examination of marriage? No—and absolutely yes. Oh, there are plenty of books about sex. But that should not prevent a look at this God-ordained gift of marriage afresh. And, yes, keep to the high ground as you strive to build a marriage that sizzles. Sex *is* high—and holy ground.

The problem with sex is hardly a lack of information. It is more an abundance of misinformation and sham.

The world today is literally saturated with sex information. Pick up almost any newspaper or magazine and you are sure to find an abundance of articles on sex. Safe sex. Premarital sex. Extramarital sex. Sex surveys. Sex research. Sex advice. The problem is hardly a lack of information. It is more an abundance of misinformation and sham. When a mylar-covered, metal-bound collection of self-indulgent erotic photographs of Madonna becomes a best-seller the day it hits the bookshelves, something is seriously wrong with our appetite. C. S. Lewis reasoned years ago that if a rare steak were slowly uncovered before a throng of clapping, shouting diners to the pounding of rhythmic music, many would suspect that group's attitude toward food might be amiss. What of our attitude about sex? Is there too much knowledge, or not enough, about what God originally intended? And if those who call the name of the Author of love do not understand His design and explain it, who in God's name will?

SEX WAS GOD'S IDEA

The church has a bad reputation where sex is concerned, and that is a shame, since it was designed and given by God Himself. Think of the diversity, the immensity, the creativity of all that God made—every bit of it good! Believers should never be ashamed to speak of that which our God has created, including sex. While Saint Augustine beautifully articulated many spiritual truths for the church, I believe he missed the boat entirely when he said, "Sex has caused the world so much trouble, I wish God had had a better idea." That is a serious libel of God, who knew exactly what He was doing in creating the beautiful area of sexual love in marriage. If He had so chosen, people could populate the earth and celebrate the covenant of marriage by the exchanging of earwax— but would *that* be a better idea? By whose standard?

To dispense knowledge without wisdom . . .is the equivalent of giving a child a hand grenade and failing to explain its explosive nature and the context of correct use.

Sex is important, a part of the fabric of life. Some say that the cornerstone of marriage is sex. While I do not believe that, I might be willing to agree with columnist Jim Sanderson that it is the apex of the marital pyramid. It is a beautiful thing, and I am thrilled to speak of it, not in some sordid, humorous, locker-room style, but in plain, biblical context, openly and unashamedly.

When I preach on this subject, I always get a few raised eyebrows or calls and letters from those who think the pulpit is not an appropriate place for a discussion of sex. Others voice their concern for the congregation and how they may be affected by what is said. To those I would simply say the only place better than the church to learn about sex would be the home. It is certainly not the secular classroom. To teach sex education apart from the Judeo-Christian context of morality is not only totally inappropriate, it is potentially damaging. To dispense knowledge without wisdom—especially to the very young—is a dangerous thing. It is the equivalent of giving a child a hand grenade and failing to explain its explosive nature and the context of correct use.

I believe children desire an understanding of the mystery of love as much, or more, than the mechanics of sex. I began to address a group of teenagers once saying, "We want to talk tonight about love." Then I began to talk a little about sex, but it was not long before one sharp teen raised a hand and said, "Pastor, we know all about sex. We want you to talk to us about love." What he was saying was, "I have a working knowledge of sex. I want help putting it into the context of love." He was right to point out my mistake of using the two words interchangeably. Sex is a part of love, but it is not always or only love.

> *There is error in isolating sex and removing it from the whole of life in two ways: by making too much of it or by making too little.*

WRONG CONCEPTS OF SEX

Sex desperately needs to be put into context today. There is error in isolating sex and removing it from the whole of life in either one of two ways: by making too much of it or by making too little. Sex is meant to be a part of the entire fabric of married life. When couples seek help for what they believe are sexual problems, they find that the difficulties are not so easily isolated. What is thought of as a sex problem is more likely than not a personality problem, a communication problem, a health problem, or a combination of these. A healthy sex life is 20 percent education and 80 percent attitude.

Some relegate the gift of sex to an instinct, believing that man, like an animal, may mate anytime, anywhere, with any kind of partner. Sex, they believe, is a bodily drive to be sated, much like hunger or thirst. The late Errol Flynn apparently believed this to some degree. He stated that his goal in life was to get as much out of women as he could. "I want to make as many women in my life as I possibly can," he said, "and the younger the better." Flynn died at the age of 50 in the company of a 17-year-old girl. He essentially said that his goal was to live like an animal, and others who see sex as only an instinct would concur. *Sex as an Instinct*

Those who attempt to make something as complex as sex into something simple and uninvolving are only fooling themselves.

> The most casual of sexual liaisons may be like some great submarine earthquake, sending its slow and un-fathomable shock waves not only into every corner of the lives of the lovers themselves, but throughout the entire nexus of family and friends, extending even to the unborn and to whole future generations. Sex is sacred ground.[3]

Some see sex as a necessary marital evil. "Sex is here to stay," they would reason, "and there's not much we can do about it." A wife with this mindset might resolve to "do her duty" to her husband, but she would find no pleasure in lovemaking and view it only as a thing to be *Sex as a Duty* endured. I hope I do not alarm anyone when I say that the idea that sex is only for procreation is not biblical. It just is not.

Sex is a God-given need meant to be satisfied in the highest, holiest, and most satisfying way: in the context of marriage. The idea that sex is wrong or perverted or unappealing is found nowhere in the Bible. Too many, especially women, have been brought up to think that sex is something to be endured rather than enjoyed, and the wife's role is simply to put up with her husband's desire for this unpleasant ritual of marriage.

> *Sex is a God-given need meant to be satisfied in the highest, holiest, and most satisfying way: in the context of marriage.*

There is no truth to the notion that as couples age they get more "spiritual" and therefore able to lay aside all sexual desires. Physical love should increase and improve, become more beautiful and more fulfilling with age. Instead of becoming routine or boring, married lovemaking can become more open and creative and satisfying as two partners age. That is part of God's plan.

The Bible says a man is to leave father and mother and cleave to his mate, so that the two might become one flesh. If the sexual relationship is a symbol of the one-flesh intimacy of marriage, then that intimacy is to involve the entire personality, not just the body. And it is a glorious goal of marriage, not a burdensome duty. Seeing sex as merely a duty is far afield of God's intent. Just a duty? Just a requirement? Oh no. Married love is a part of the excitement and thrill and romance of life's most intimate human bond.

Sex as a Bargaining Chip

To use sex in a manipulative way is completely out of bounds. This is perhaps the cheapest estimation of all of married love. For a wife to manipulate her husband by consenting to or witholding sex based on his behavior is to place herself in the position of a prostitute. I know that is a harsh word—but it is a straight one. And the woman who continually ups the ante on sex may find after a time that her husband has begun to look for a better bargain. Again—do not misunderstand. It is never right for a husband or wife to be unfaithful, no matter what the circumstances of their marriage may be. There is no excuse for unfaithfulness. There is no excuse for a man not to show affection toward his wife. And there is no excuse for a woman to refuse to meet her husband's basic need for sexual fulfillment.

Remember, every other need a husband has can be met by someone else. But his wife is the only one who can rightly satisfy him sexually. No one else can do that. The Bible is very clear in this area—painfully so.

> Now concerning the things about which you wrote. It is good for a man not to touch a woman. But because of immoralities, let each man have his own wife, and let each woman have her own husband. Let the husband fulfill his duty to his wife, and likewise also the wife to her husband. The wife does not have authority over her own body, but the husband does; and likewise the husband does not have authority over his own body, but the wife does. (1 Cor. 7:1-4)

Husbands and wives will not hit the mark 100 percent of the time, because even the best person is far from perfect.

WHAT THE MAKER INTENDED

Sex is not simply a duty. It is not a manipulative weapon. It is not merely an animal instinct. But what *did* God have in mind when He conceived this tremendous drive in man? What did He intend His creation to be?

Before anything else, sex is a gift. It is God-planned, God-designed, and God-given. It did not originate with Hugh Hefner or Madonna or Errol Flynn. It began in the heart and the mind of God. He looked at the man, Adam, that He had created, and decided that it was not good for him to be alone. So He made a woman to be his helper, his partner, his mate. His intent was that they become one flesh through the intimate act of marriage. And this is the same symbol that is used to depict our relationship to Jesus Christ.

Before anything else, sex is a gift. It is God-planned, God designed, and God given.

The Bible says Adam *knew* Eve; the Hebrew word connotes sexual intimacy. The same Hebrew word is used to describe the way to know God in Jesus Christ. That is the kind of intimacy believers are to experience with the living God! And in both cases, it is good and sacred and holy and precious. But as with any gift given by God, Satan desires to distort, misdirect, and misuse it. A lack of understanding of the true nature of this beautiful and sacred gift plays right into the deceiver's hand.

Some in their childhood can remember that a mother and father's relationship fell far short of what God planned. Perhaps the mother withheld sex or used it as a subtle weapon against her mate. Or maybe a cloudy kind of negativism surrounded the whole area of sex. Questions were taboo. No references were made. No explanations were given. Children were reprimanded for their curiousity: "You're too young to know about that! Who put such dirty thoughts in your head? We'll tell you all you need to know when it is time."

The time to speak of sex is when children ask. The secret is to respond on the level of the child's questions. I'm reminded of the story of a little boy who ran in to his mother saying "Mommy, Mommy, where did I come from?"

She grabbed the refrigerator door to steady herself, took a deep breath, reminding herself that she had read a dozen books in preparation for this moment, and had the tools to do it right. "Well, Bobby, when two people love each other very much like your daddy and I do, they get married, and when they get married . . ."

He was impatient. This sounded like it was going to be one of those long drawn-out answers. "Mommy, just tell me! I've got to know. Where did I come from?"

She started over. "Let me back up. First, there were these birds. Oh, and bees, too. They were flying from flower to flower and . . ."

He couldn't stand it. "Mommy, what about me? Where did I come from? My friend Billy says he came from Atlanta. Where did I come from?"

It is so important to understand the level of the questions children ask. A good response might be, "That's a good question, son. What made you think of it today?" Then form your answer on that level. The answers need to be good ones, because directly and indirectly, children receive answers about sex that are neither wholesome nor correct. A little girl might hear older women talking about childbirth, saying something like, "Let me just tell you, I was in labor for 29 hours and it was the worst pain of my life. Then the doctor didn't even make it on time." She listens to one "horror story" after another, and begins to think that the worst thing that could happen to her would be to get pregnant and deliver a child.

Later in life she marries and because those childhood fears are somehow connected to her feelings about lovemaking, she has tremendous problems adjusting to this aspect of married life. Exposure to extramarital sex—affairs by either parent—are also deeply damaging to a child's view of sexuality. Then too, children hear half-truths and total untruths about sex outside the home—unfortunately today, sometimes even in the secular school classroom.

If adults view sex as a gift from God—who gives only good gifts, by the way—children will come to view it the same way as they mature. God creates men and women with a sexual appetite—a desire. Then within the bonds of marriage, He provides a way for that desire to be satisfied that is both pure and pleasurable. What a wise and wonderful giver He is!

Sex, too, is an art. Any husband or wife who thinks he or she has this whole mystery figured out has only demonstrated their ignorance. If a painter knew all there was to know about light and color and form, could he not produce a masterpiece every time he picked up his brush? Why not? Because the intangible of his art is creativity, and without it, anything he turns out is only a mechanical exercise. Great sex, like great art, is a product of inspired creativity, and adjustments are made all along the way.

> *Great sex, like great art, is a product of inspired creativity, and adjustments are made all along the way.*

LEARNING TO ADAPT

A couple planned an off-season, mid-February vacation to Hawaii. They saved their money and found just the right travel offer. Tickets purchased, they bought new summer clothes—shorts, tropical-print shirts, sandals, sunglasses, and hats. They pictured themselves on Waikiki Beach in the moonlight and imagined the scents of wild hibiscus and orchids.

Finally the day came. They boarded the 747 for paradise, but instead of arriving hours later in Hawaii, their plane touched down in Anchorage, Alaska. It was 32 degrees below zero. It had been snowing for four months straight. Their plane was in need of repairs, and the airport was quickly shut down. They were put up indefinitely in a small but cozy cabin on the side of a rocky ridge.

At this point, they were faced with choices. They could wear their beach clothes, walk out in the snow, and freeze to death. They could huddle around the fire and be miserable. They could yearn for the moonlit nights on the beach, and spend their entire time in Alaska pouting and arguing: "No one here can hula. I hate soup. I wanted fish. It's all your fault."

Or, they could buy some winter clothes and learn to cross-country ski. They could snuggle by a crackling fire. They could enjoy the wildlife of their snowy outpost—and delight in an unexpected second honeymoon. And that is what they did.

In marriage, as in discount travel, adjustments must be made. Sexual love in marriage is a gift. It is an art. And it should always be a celebration. Listen to these words of celebration from two ancient lovers:

> My beloved is dazzling and ruddy. Outstanding among ten thousand. His head is like gold, pure gold; his locks are like clusters of dates, and black as a raven. His eyes are like doves, beside streams of water, bathed in milk, and reposed in their setting. His cheeks are like a bed of balsam, banks of sweet-scented herbs; his lips are lilies, dripping with liquid myrrh. His hands are rods of gold set with beryl; his abdomen is carved ivory inlaid with sapphires. His legs are pillars of alabaster set on pedestals of pure gold; his appearance is like Lebanon, choice as the cedars. His mouth is full of sweetness and wholly desirable. This is my beloved and this is my friend. (Song of Sol. 5:10-16)

Do you get the idea that this is a woman who is deeply attracted to her husband and celebrates his sexuality? And her husband reciprocates those feelings:

> How beautiful are your feet in sandals, O prince's daughter! The curves of your hips are like jewels, the work of the hands of an artist. Your navel is like a round goblet which never lacks mixed wine; your belly is like a heap of wheat fenced in with lilies. Your breasts are like two fawns, twins of a gazelle. Your neck is like a tower of ivory, your eyes like pools in Heshbon by the

gate of Bath-Rabbim; your nose is like the tower of Lebanon, which faces toward Damascus. Your head crowns you like Carmel, and the flowing locks of your head are like purple threads; the king is captivated by your tresses. How beautiful and how delightful you are, my love, with all your charms! Your stature is like a palm tree, and your breasts are like its clusters. I said, "I will climb the palm tree, and I will take hold of its stalks." And may your breasts be like clusters of the vine, and the fragrance of your breath like apples, and your mouth like the best wine! It goes down smoothly for my beloved, flowing gently through the lips of those who fall asleep. (Song of Sol. 7:1-9)

These lovers know the celebratory aspect of sex as God intended it. They understand sex as excitement, pleasure, desire, laughter, and celebration. And this sex-saturated society has missed it, settling instead for Satan's counterfeited version of the real thing. What a tragedy. What a loss.

You Are Not Your Own

If all those who read this book were given an informal survey and asked whether or not they believed the Bible, there would be almost total unanimity. I believe the vast majority would say, "Yes, I believe the Bible." If I went further and asked whether those believed every word of the Bible, I still think the answer would be good. Then if I queried about the authority of the Bible, most who answered affirmatively from the beginning would concur, "Yes, I believe in the authority of God's Word." What about its infallibility? "Oh, yes . . . " If I asked those Bible-believing faithful whether or not the Scriptures were a rule and a guide for their lives, I can imagine them saying, "Yes, sir. That's what I believe."

Let me tell you how much of the Bible people really believe. Do you know how much? People believe exactly the amount of it that they *practice*. That's how much they believe—no more, and no less. God's Word says that a wife does not have authority over her own body, but her husband does, and conversely, that a husband does not have authority over his own body, rather his wife. That means when they decide to marry, they give their body over to their spouse. They no longer belong to themselves in the physical sense.

> *People believe exactly as much of the Bible as they practice.*

That certainly changes the way you look at sex. You do not own your body. I do not own my body. In marriage, two become one flesh, and the basic desire is to please one's mate. The husband wants, more than anything else, to please his wife in every way. The wife wants, more than anything else, to please her husband in every way. "Do you mean," you might ask, "just because I'm married I'm going to throw my life away and give it all to my mate?" That is right. Now you are beginning to understand. If you did not know this when you married, you made your decision with inadequate information. If you are married, I dare you to live under this biblical principle and see what will happen, not just in your sex life, but in the totality of your union. That's strong, isn't it? Mark Twain was right on the money when he said his problem with the Bible was not in deciphering the passages he did not understand, but in applying those that he did. Most of us would have to agree.

If people do not own their bodies, then the sharing of them in married love should be a habit, in the best sense of the word. If a husband and a wife agree to abstain from sex temporarily for a spiritual reason, that is fine. But this arrangement should not go on too long, because to neglect sex with one's spouse for too long is to place him or her in a vulnerable position where temptation is concerned. It would almost be a waste of ink to belabor this point. That these temptations exist is too obvious to argue. If you have ventured past your own driveway this week you know what they are. Neglect leads to temptation just as morning leads to noon.

Do you know why most affairs take place? It is so simple. Most affairs happen because people believe they can receive from another person that which they are not receiving from their mate. A man strays because he believes somehow that he will find in this other one what he is not finding at home with his wife. Often it is sexual fulfillment. A wife strays because she hopes that another man will provide for her what her husband will not. Often it is affection.

> *To neglect sex with one's spouse for too long is to place him or her in a vulnerable position where temptation is concerned.*

A beautiful woman began seeing a marriage counselor. Her walk, her dress, her smile were real attention-getters. She was extremely attractive. "I'm falling in love with a man in my office," she said. "We haven't had sexual relations, but I'm falling in love with him." What did the object of her desire look like? "Oh," she said, "if you met him you would think him the homeliest, most unattractive man you've ever seen. Truthfully, most would say he was ugly. You would never pick him out as someone I'd be attracted to." Why, then? "Well," she replied, "my husband is so cold, so hard, so indifferent, dogmatic, arrogant. He refuses to communicate with me or try to understand me. I've reached out to him, and done everything I know to do, but he is beyond reach as far as I'm concerned." What about the gentleman at the office? Her eyes lit up immediately. "He doesn't imagine that I'm even interested in him because he is so ordinary. But he's sensitive and warm, he listens to me, encourages me, and is genuinely interested in how I feel. I'm afraid of what I'm flirting with. I know it is sin, but I'm just so hungry for understanding and kindness and communication."

How sad that a wife's need for affection is met by a near stranger when it should be the habit of her husband to do so. How equally sad when a man's need for sexual fulfillment is met outside the ideal atmosphere of marriage because it is not the habit of his wife to give herself to him in this way. If a wife can identify with "Tired, in Lincoln, Nebraska," or a husband knows his wife would agree, changes need to be made. Wives and husbands, begin to build a dynamic sexual relationship with your mate that is exciting to you, encouraging to your children, and glorifying to God. That was His plan from the beginning!

QUESTIONS FOR FURTHER REFLECTION

1. Wife, how would you respond to the letter from "Tired in Lincoln, Nebraska"? Do you agree or disagree with the statement ". . . most women get very little physical satisfaction out of sex: they just go through the motions because they want to do something for the men they love"?

2. How does using sex as a "bargaining chip" affect a marriage? Is it ever right?

3. How might neglecting physical lovemaking in marriage place a husband and wife in a vulnerable position?

4. Do you primarily see sex as a duty, a gift, an art, or a celebration? Discuss your answer with your mate.

8

CAN WE TALK?

A Wife Needs:
Meaningful Communication

THEY SIT ON A LEDGE OVER THE SINK in our kitchen: two wooden figures, a man and a woman, bought by my wife at a country store some years ago. Each of them bears a cryptic message. His reads: "When Daddy ain't happy, nobody cares." Hers reads: "When Momma ain't happy, ain't *nobody* happy." While the implications of these two statements are probably too deep and profound to comment on further, I will say that a husband meeting his wife's basic needs in marriage is critical to marital happiness—hers and his!

What makes a wife happy? Affection is likely the number one need a woman looks to her husband to fill—but meaningful communication runs a close second. In his book, *A Different Drum*, Scott Peck describes a marital "pseudo-community" in which a husband and wife grow further and further apart, living lives that are parallel but seldom intersect in any meaningful way. Just because a couple live together under the same roof, share the same bed, eat the same groceries, and parent the same children does not mean they are intimately connected. I know too many people who would say "That's us!" or "That describes our marriage."

YOU'VE GOT TO WANT TO

I am convinced good communication in marriage begins with desire. Most women have a built-in desire to communicate in a meaningful way with their spouse. It is a little less natural for men, but by no means out of the question. Both must begin with the desire to share with one another in a way that is open and honest and vital and real. It all begins with desire. If a man has the desire to deep-sea fish, he will find the time, find a boat, find the right equipment, and go. If he has the desire to be the number one salesman in his company, he will study the market, keep up with his customers, know his product, and hit the streets, day after day.

> *Good communication in marriage begins with desire.*

If a man desires to meet the needs of his wife and give her security—if he wants her to be his best friend, his partner and confidant, he will make intimate communication with her a priority. Not conversation, but communication—the intimate, gut-level, honest exchange of thoughts, dreams, ideas, and goals. Communication will not be easy for him, but it is important for a marriage that is alive, a marriage that sizzles. For that kind of relationship, communication is ground zero.

Women excel at this, and by comparison, men are novices. Did you know that studies have been done of newborn babies that show that females move their lips hundreds of times more than do the males? Research on preschool children has shown that almost 100 percent of the sounds made by girls are word-related, but only 68 percent of the sounds boys made could be tied to literal words. The remaining 32 percent of the sounds little boys made were noises—truck noises, airplane noises, gun noises. Some wives would say their husbands have not advanced much beyond those playground sounds of "Hmmm" and "Ohhmmm . . ."!

Physiologically, women are more prone to be good communicators. More women than men are right-brain oriented, and it is the right

The failure to listen might be the biggest hindrance of all to marital communication.

hemisphere of the brain that controls the emotions, feelings, creativity, and artistic impulses. Generally, men are more left-brain oriented, which controls the logical, analytical aspects of behavior. Men are more prone to be linear thinkers with thought processes which move from A to B to C. Women tend to be global thinkers, their minds can move over an amazing array of details at once, seeing the relationships between them with ease.

People like to do the things that they are naturally good at; they gravitate toward them, and enjoy them. The things that are more difficult tend to be avoided, but no one can afford to avoid cultivating intimate communication with a mate, whether it comes easily or not. Women by nature are the more gifted communicators, but men can be taught, if they do not fall prey to what I call communication killers.

Communication Killers (and How to Avoid Them)

Intimacy begins with the ears. Now I realize that might sound a little strange, but it is absolutely true. The *failure to listen* might be the biggest hindrance of all to intimate communication. Real listening begins when a husband and wife decide to devote themselves to studying the innermost thoughts and feelings of their mate. This is holy ground—and listening is the doorway to all that lies beyond. There is little more irritating than the feeling that no one is listening. One woman said, "My husband always seems to take a pen out of his pocket and play with it while I am talking to him." Another said, "He never looks at me. He won't put down his paper and make eye contact." Still another complained, "He always answers me with some humorous aside, or tries to change the subject if I'm upset. Or even worse, he tries to complete my sentences, thinking he knows exactly what I am about to say." That kind of half-hearted listening would be discouraging, would it not?

Next time your spouse begins to open his or her heart, try this. Lean in. Physically lean forward and engage your mind. You are being invited into the holy ground of another soul. Respond verbally in a way that encourages further communication. "Hmmm, I see what you mean." Ask for clarification. A simple "What I hear you saying is . . . Is that right?" lets your spouse know you are not only listening—you want to get it right. You want to understand. If you are unsure you do understand, back up and try again. "Could you say that another way? I'm not sure I know what you mean."

Listening goes beyond just hearing the words. A wife seems upset. Her husband says, "Honey, is anything wrong?" She hesitates, then blurts out, "I guess not . . . I'm just a little low today—a little down, that's all." Hearing her "I guess not," he moves to the next thing: "That's good. I wonder if the Astros are on tonight?" Did he miss something? You bet he did. He missed an open door to real communication. He heard the words, but he failed to understand. A better response would have been, "You really are down, aren't you? How can I help?" She allowed her husband to see just a little bit of her heart, and he declined the invitation to further revelation.

A husband comes home and says, "We had a birthday party at work today for Bob. He's 27. You know, in a few months I'll be 30. That sounds really old." His wife, half listening, responds, "I think it's great that you celebrate your birthdays at the office. I guess you'll have a party soon, too." She heard "birthday party," but the key words were actually "that sounds really old," weren't they? He was concerned about growing older and there was invitation in those words, but she missed the moment.

> *Trust is like "money in the bank" in a marriage. There must be a reasonable amount of it on deposit to ensure the security of a marital union.*

And finally, remember what is said in communication with your mate. I would be embarrassed to tell you how many times JoBeth has asked me stop on the way home for something and I've forgotten. Listen to your mate as if you expected a quiz later—you might get one! The truth is that we usually recall what is important to us. I do not know too many men who have forgotten that their fishing buddies were picking them up at 4:30 in the morning, do you?

Although the failure to listen is one communication killer, *lying* is lethal to marital communication as well. Trust is like "money in the bank" in a marriage. There must be a reasonable amount of it on deposit to ensure the security of a marital union. Trust is essential in any intimate relationship—and lying destroys it quicker than just about anything else. God is never pleased with it.

A worthless person, a wicked man, is the one who walks with a false mouth . . . . There are six things which the Lord hates, yes, seven which are an abomination to Him: haughty eyes, a lying tongue, and hands that shed innocent blood, a heart that devises wicked plans, feet that run rapidly to evil, a false witness who utters lies, and one who spreads strife among brothers (Prov. 6:12, 16-19).

In one sense, all are born liars. No one had to be taught to lie, did they? None have had formal training in the intricacies of deception; all are self-taught. Unfortunately, many born liars improve vastly with age, until they would rather lie than tell the truth. I know a man who is a wonderful storyteller. He spins a story so beautifully that when he is done, all within earshot would say "It's absolutely true." The trouble is that he embellishes—blows things up a little larger than life to make sure that they're seen. He'll take something he's seen or read and apply it to his own experience, or someone else's. And he is fascinating. You are at the edge of your seat saying, "This is incredible." (And upon examination, that is exactly what it is!) The trouble is in forgetting how to tell the truth—and why it is important to do so. Born liars can become extremely skillful with regular practice, so skilled that truth and fiction begin to merge, making it impossible to discern where one ends and the other begins.

Another kind of liar is what I call the don't-rock-the-boat liar. The operative philosophy here might be "she can't get mad about what she doesn't know." The problem with "don't rock the boat" liars is that when the truth finally comes out, instead of smooth seas, it's typhoon time! The wife of a "don't rock the boat liar" might come to her husband and say, "Could you mail these bills when you get to the office this morning?" And her husband would respond, "Oh, sure. No problem." Then on the way in to work, he slips the bills over the sun visor in the car and never thinks about them again. The next day is Friday. She doesn't ask. He doesn't remember. Then on Saturday she says, "You remembered to mail those bills, right?"

"Of course I did," he lies. "Did you think I was going to forget?" Then on Monday morning, he takes them out and drops them in the mail saying, "No harm done. She'll never know." And she may not—this time. But there will be another, because the habit of lying is being established in the name of marital peace.

Another variation of the "don't-rock-the-boat" liar is the husband who lies to shield his wife from realities he believes are too difficult for her, but are truly disturbing him. I know a man who was a very respected banker—a church member, a good man, an outstanding citizen—but who lived a double life. For years he had gambled in secret and had amassed enormous debt, owing hundreds of thousands of dollars to bookies across the country. Only when his debts were discovered publicly did his wife and family learn that he had been struggling for years.

It is a tragedy to lose all that you own, all that you have built through the years, as this man learned. But it is an even greater tragedy to lose those that you love most in the process because you have lied to them and shut them out. He sought to shield them. He did not want them to be worried. And when the truth came out, the weight of the waves did not just rock the boat—they obliterated it.

Limited disclosure is a variation of marital dishonesty. Lies are not actually told, but the whole of the truth is withheld for a variety of reasons. The root of limited disclosure is usually selfishness, and it is illustrated no better than in the biblical account of a couple named Ananias and Sapphira.

But a certain man named Ananias, with his wife Sapphira, sold a piece of property, and kept back some of the price for himself, with his wife's full knowledge, and bringing a portion of it, he laid it at the apostles' feet. But Peter said, "Ananias, why has Satan filled your heart to lie to the Holy Spirit, and to keep back some of the price of the land? While it remained unsold did it not remain your own? And after it was sold, was it not under your control? Why is it that you have conceived this deed in your heart? You have not lied to men, but to God. And as he heard these words, Ananias fell down and breathed his last (Acts 5:1–5).

Knowledge is power—and the willful withholding of information with the intent to deceive is the moral equivalent of lying, as this example so graphically illustrates. Many have become masters of rationalization, but God's standards have not changed, have they? He still hates a lying tongue and a heart that devises wicked plans. He always will.

> *The willful withholding of information with intent to deceive is the moral equivalent of lying.*

Not only is communication between spouses in the right way important, doing so at the right time is critical. *Poor timing* is a communication killer. A seated dinner party with twelve invited guests is not the appropriate time to tell your spouse you are tired of her lasagna. When your seventh grader has a gash in her knee that looks like it requires stitches, I do not recommend you stop everything for a heart-to-heart. When both of you are weary after a long day, it is unlikely that you will make much headway in a detailed analysis of your finances, your in-laws, your sex life, or anything else, for that matter.

Do you know what it takes for a 140-pound shortstop to hit a smoking fastball over a 400-foot fence? Timing. And if spouses are going to be home-run hitters in marital communication, they will have to develop a sense of timing. So often a morning person marries a night person. The one who hits the ground running at 5:30 a.m. is exhausted at 8:30 or 9:00 at night—they've had it, but the night person is just beginning to hit their stride! This is complicated even further by the fact that the early morning and late evening hours are those most couples spend with one another, so timing is important. "Like apples of gold in settings of silver," wrote King Solomon, "is a word spoken in right circumstances" (Prov. 25:11).

So listen to your mates. Tell the truth—and tell it completely. Communicate your thoughts and feelings at the appropriate time. But even after doing all these things right, a final communication killer can destroy a marriage over time: *terminal words*.

Terminal words are pronouncements that leave no room for retreat, concession, apology, or invitation. They are *last* words. They sound something like this: "You'll never change." "I'll never do that." "You are totally wrong." "I told you so." "You always forget." "I never should have married you." "I won't forgive you." "I am absolutely sure." And then the phrase Ronald Reagan made famous in his debate with Walter Mondale: "There you go again."

Terminal words have the effect of burying a live marriage in concrete. They bring communication to a grinding stop, and all momentum is lost. It is enormous work to overcome the sheer weight of terminal words and begin to move toward one another again.

> *Terminal words leave no room for retreat, concession, apology or invitation. They are last words.*

Why is this so? Because there is a power in words, and every combination of letters and sounds holds within it the possibility to build or to destroy. As Frederick Buechner has said, "To put into words our anger, our love, our forgiveness, our desire, is, even if we were never to act upon our words, to affect powerfully both the lives of the ones we are addressing and our own lives. Words are dangerous because for better or worse they are so powerful."[1] It is not enough to strive to eliminate terminal words; they must be replaced with words that invite communication instead. Words like: "Would it be all right if I talked to you about . . . ?" "I feel like . . . " "I wonder if . . . " "I hope we can . . . " These are phrases that leave the door ajar for further expression, and that is critical.

The most frightening sound in a troubled marriage is silence.

Do you know the most frightening sound in a troubled marriage? It is silence. Men respond to marital difficulty with anger and withdrawal. Women tend to respond with depression and withdrawal. Terminal words spoken when one or both partners are angry or depressed are usually followed by a lengthy silence that gets harder to break as time goes on. I am less concerned about a marriage where the partners frequently argue than I am about one in which they never speak. Even if you are angry with one another, do your best to keep talking.

Two Helpful Stances for Husbands

What I am about to suggest may not be very popular or sound too sophisticated. I realize entire books have been written on marital communication, and we will not exhaust the subject here. But I believe there are two stances a wise husband will learn and employ in communicating with his wife—especially when she is troubled. People communicate for many reasons: to understand one another, to inform one another, and also to comfort one another. Paul told the Galatians to "bear one another's burdens, and thus fulfill the law of Jesus Christ" (Gal. 6:2). In this area of comfort men so often fall short. Notice Paul said "bear one another's burdens," and not "solve one another's problems." There is a difference, and it is key.

The apostle Paul said we are to "bear one another's burdens," not "solve one another's problems.

When a wife is sad or upset or depressed, what does a husband normally do? Most men begin by asking her questions, then seize the first opportunity to jump in and save the day with wise counsel and amazingly efficient problem-solving ability. That's because men are conditioned to be condensers. They take information, evaluate it, condense it to a manageable (translate that "fixable" in this case) kernel, and then deal with it. And men see this tendency as something that should instantly bring calm and comfort to their wives.

It might, too, except for the fact that women are amplifiers. They expand on the obvious, look at it from all angles, delve into the details. They don't want a solution so much as expression. And that is why husbands need to learn "the bucket stance." It is what it sounds like. When a wife is angry, upset, or emotional, a wise husband will simply "hold the bucket" until she is done expressing her emotions. No solutions. No suggestions. No logic. Just hold the bucket. Resist the impulse to get to the bottom line and give simple remedies. Sometimes the answers are not simple to a woman who sees life from all its angles. Sometimes her feelings are beyond his depth to understand. She does not need him to make sense of it all—but she does need someone who will hold the bucket.

The other stance men need to learn is what I call "the mirror stance." As much as I dislike admitting it at times, a mirror is basically honest. It reflects the image as it is seen: no changes, no enhancements, just unadorned reality. By using a mirror, we are able to make adjustments in what is seen, improving on the way things are. When a husband adopts the mirror stance with his wife, he clarifies things for her—he gives her the gift of perspective and the feeling that she discovered it herself.

How does a man become a mirror for his wife? By hearing her words (and the feelings behind them) and serving them back to her in a way that lets her know he understood. For example:

> *Wife:* I can't believe my boss questioned the validity of our proposal in front of the client. He has known what was in the plan for weeks.
>
> *Husband:* You're upset that he didn't voice his concerns to you before the presentation, aren't you?
>
> *Wife:* Yes, especially when there were at least half a dozen times he could have, before today. It made us look unprepared.
>
> *Husband:* It must have been frustrating to you, especially since I know how hard you worked to have everything in place for today.
>
> *Wife:* I've spent hours and hours going over every question they might have. I didn't expect the first one to come from our own executive group! It was embarrassing, to say the least.
>
> *Husband:* I guess you felt like you had a whole room full of people to win over at that point, didn't you?

If the conversation continues in this way, the wife can process her jumbled emotions without her husband telling her what she should have done or how he would have handled things. Her need for expression will be met as a result of his mirror stance. Then, and only then, will she be ready to hear another perspective on what took place.

Communication in the Garden   Once upon a time, there was a couple who enjoyed intimate communication with one another as a way of life. This was before courses on "How to Talk to Anyone About Practically Anything" were developed. This was before counselors and psychologists taught us relating skills. And this was before sin.

But when that first act of disobedience occurred, it set in motion a series of deceptions whose repercussions are still felt. Satan, disguised as a serpent, convinced Eve that God had not communicated truthfully the results of eating the forbidden fruit. She believed him, and she ate. She encouraged her husband to eat, and he did. Disobedience begat shame, and the beautiful, open communication they once had was gone. They covered themselves, hiding from one another and from God. Then they lied to Him.

The next generation did not fare much better. Brother murdered brother and then tried to deny responsibility. Jealousy was born. Abraham, recipient of the covenant promises of God, was a great man of faith, but he resorted to dishonesty easily enough when he believed his wife's beauty would compromise his own safety. What did he do? He told people she was his sister. His son Isaac did likewise years later with his own wife, Rebekah. Isaac had a son, Jacob, whose very name meant "liar, cheat, deceiver." He started early, lying to his brother and his father and stealing the birthright that belonged to his brother.

> *Broken relationships, lies, and half-truths are our heritage from the garden until now. But so is the desire to know and be known in an intimate way.*

Jacob's sons sold their own brother Joseph into slavery, then lied about what they had done. Broken relationships, lies, and half-truths are our heritage from the garden until now. But so is the desire to know and be known in a deep and intimate way; this is a part of the very fabric of our souls as well. Obviously, true intimacy is difficult to find. One scholar has said it is as hard to find as real gold. But prospectors do find gold, even today. And many people manage to find the intimacy they seek through real, honest communication with their mates. When they do, they are rich because to know and be known by the one you love above all others *is* better than gold.

QUESTIONS 1. Do you agree or disagree with the statement, "Inti-
FOR macy begins with the ears"? How has failing to listen to
FURTHER your mate affected your communication?
REFLECTION 2. Which of these "communication killers" has done
the most damage in your home? Failure to listen? Lying?
Limited disclosure? Poor timing? Terminal words?
Make a concentrated effort to eliminate it.

3. Husband, have you learned how to "hold the
bucket," or "mirror" your wife's words? Explain these
concepts to your wife and ask her which would be most
helpful to her.

9

THE FAMILY THAT PLAYS TOGETHER

A Husband Needs:
Companionship

Then the LORD God said, "It is not good for the man to be alone" (Gen. 2:18).

"This is my beloved and this is my friend" (Song of Sol. 5:16).

JIM AND DORIS WERE CASUAL ACquaintances who worked in the same downtown office building. One day as they waited for an elevator they found time for more than just a prefunctory, "Hi, how are you?" Amazingly enough, they quickly discovered they had mutual friends. On the spur of the moment, Jim said, "I'm going out for barbecue. Would you like to come along?" She didn't hesitate. "Sure, I love barbecue. Sounds great."

So these two nice single adults went out to lunch and both enjoyed it. They soon found that they had much in common and shared many interests. Jim learned that Doris was a jogger. Thinking that lunch was going particularly well, he took a measured risk: "I'm going jogging today after work. If you have clothes with you, why don't we jog together?" She said she needed someone to jog with, and that she would be thrilled to do so.

After work Jim and Doris jogged, and soon they were having lunch and jogging on a regular basis. Lunches out and jogging evolved into a dating relationship, based at least in part on their similar interests. One day in late fall, Jim said he had tickets to the University of Texas-Texas A&M football game—a traditionally hard-fought and always well-attended meeting of Southwest Conference rivals. Would she like to go? "I'd be delighted," she told him. "I haven't been to a game in ages, but I do enjoy watching on televison." So they went—and they had a tremendous time watching the game together. Jim was exhuberant over her obvious interest in his favorite sport, and she listened with great attentiveness as he explained the finer points of gridiron strategy.

A short time later, when the couple planned to jog on a Saturday afternoon, Jim's car was in need of minor repairs. So he called Doris and said he really needed the time to work on it. "That's okay," she said. "I jogged yesterday. I'll come over and help you instead." They spent another glorious afternoon with one another—Jim under the hood making unintelligible noises, and Doris handing him tools as they were needed. The repairs went so smoothly there was time to wash and wax the car when they were done. Jim was impressed. *Even fixing the car is fun with Doris,* he thought to himself. *You know, this might just be the best date we've ever had.*

Neither Jim nor Doris had ever been in a relationship where they did so many things together with the person they were dating. It was fabulous, really. It wasn't long before Jim proposed, and Doris eagerly accepted. They had a small wedding, then took off for a honeymoon in the mountains, hiking, talking, dreaming of the wonderful future they would build, and thrilling in their uninterrupted time together.

Marriage was a little more complex than dating, but it was good. Their first six months went by in a flash, and both of them settled into married life. One day Doris got up and said, "You know, sweetheart, my knee is really bothering me. I think I'll skip jogging today. You go on without me." Another football season rolled around, and Jim reminded her they had tickets again for the big game. It was, after all, the one where they really knew they were on to something good; he was certain she would want to go and re-experience that thrill. "Oh, the game," she responded. "I'd like to go, of course, but I've got some reading to catch up on. Why don't you ask one of the guys and make a day of it?"

Their first football season as a married couple—and they hadn't seen one game together! Then Doris began to leave brochures around for the ballet and the opera—interests Jim had never heard her mention before. "Oh, I've always loved opera," she said when he asked her about her new hobby. "And the ballet, too." When an exhibit of Spanish Renaissance painters came to town, he discovered she liked to visit museums as well—something that was never mentioned in their dating experience. What he learned from this outing was that museums were very . . . quiet. And that there was no loud talking. And that while applause was the correct way to acknowledge the beauty of a 32-yard off-tackle run, you just sort of nodded when you saw a nice painting.

Before long, Doris stopped jogging altogether. And she couldn't care less about routine car maintenance. He was lucky if she put gas in every other time. Another football season came and went without her attendance at one single game. But she did join the guild of the local performing arts complex, and she was appointed to several committees that promoted arts awareness. She made many friends among the women she met in these activities, and Jim began to pal around with his football buddies. He even started jogging with another man from his office. Then one night they discussed where to take her parents to dinner, and Doris delivered the final shocking news: "Let's go anywhere but the barbecue place. I can't stand barbecue!"

SHARED EXPERIENCES There will always be a certain amount of unintentional deception in dating relationships. Both parties want to please, want to put their best foot forward. Sometimes they agree eagerly to things that are not particularly appealing because they want to be with one another. This is normal. You might even argue that there is nothing wrong with a marriage where there are no shared interests, but both husband and wife pursue their own interests alone or with other friends. Perhaps not. But some of the high moments in life come from shared experience.

> *A man's need for recreational companionship is second only to his desire for sexual fulfillment.*

According to Dr. Harley's observations in *His Needs Her Needs*, a man's need for recreational companionship is second only to his desire for sexual fulfillment. On the surface, this seems a little odd, but when we remember that women cement relationships with talk and men bond by shared experience, it makes more sense. A man knows others and allows himself to be known in the context of activity.

The courtship experience of Doris and Jim is not atypical. According to sociologist Annette Lawson, author of *Adultery: An Analysis of Love and Betrayal*, men and women use talking, self-expression, and self-disclosure to draw close emotionally before marriage, but after marriage, they begin to relate by reading "his and hers scripts." She still relies on verbal expression for intimacy, but he shifts to a reliance on *shared activity* to achieve closeness. It has been said countless times that the family that prays together, stays together, but I would add another dimension to that and say that the family that *plays* together stays together.

There are just so many hours in the day, and you choose how you will spend each of them. Out of necessity, some will be spent working, some maintaining the home, some in school, and so on. What is left is called "discretionary time." If a mate chooses to spend all of this time away from the one who is to be his best friend and pursues private interests, the marriage partners will begin to slowly drift apart. Shared activity, play, and laughter can improve even the best of relationships.

Do you and your mate have a recreational pursuit that you both genuinely enjoy, and do you share in that activity together on a regular basis? Certainly a husband may have interests that his wife does not share, and vice versa, but is there one thing that you both like to do together? If there is not, find something! Let each partner make a lengthy list of the things they enjoy. Do not put anything on the list that you would not like to do fairly often—and list as many different things as you can. Compare lists and find at least one thing that you both like to do, and then do it!

I like basketball. I like it a lot. JoBeth and I have three sons who played basketball, and we have watched many games together. If our boys had not played, I do not know that she would have been interested in the game at all, but I would have. My wife is an artist. She paints and shows her work and takes classes in art. She is very talented, but my interest in art begins and ends with JoBeth. A short time ago we were in southern California together. We spent an entire afternoon walking from art gallery to art gallery—and she loved it! My idea of a great way to spend a day in the Los Angeles area would be to watch the UCLA Bruins practice, but that is not what we did. We each have our own interests, but we have things that are fun to do together, too. Recently, we bought a pool table so that we could both learn to play pool.

At this point some men are probably thinking, *I'm not sure my wife could ever hit one of those little quail.* Some women are saying to themselves, *He'll never know a* pas de duex *from a pass-the-mustard.* Maybe not. But probably the two of you could designate something as your "sport," and learn to love it together. Maybe antique collecting. Or camping. Or sign language. Or parachuting. Who knows? On the other hand, if there is something you do for recreation that your mate simply cannot abide, you need to think seriously about quitting. Your marriage is more important than stock car racing or dog training or craftmaking. Turn the time you used to spend on that passion to another one—spending mutually enjoyable time with your husband or wife, who is to be your best friend.

> *Business relationships are frequently helped by recreational companionship . . . Why not a marriage?*

The benefits of recreational companionship are not difficult to understand in non-marital relationships. Business relationships are frequently helped by it. Corporate golf tournaments, hunting trips, fishing trips—all center on the sharing of mutually satisfying recreational experiences to strengthen work ties. Key customers or clients are included in these kinds of activities, and while the "deals" are culminated in board rooms and offices, the relationships they are based on are often cemented on the links, the lake, or elsewhere. Why not a marriage?

The sharing of these peak experiences and enjoyable moments with a mate can strengthen and nurture the marriage relationship, too. When a husband or wife consistently misses out on something which gives the other one pleasure, a serious mistake is made. Be involved! Be a part! Learn the value of hours shared in play with one another.

The truth that "the family that plays together stays together" would not be so critical if families were just automatically self-sustaining. But they are not. I hardly need to press the point that families are in trouble today. If your own family is not, you need not look far to find one that is. Infidelity, substance abuse, addiction, divorce, and latch-key children all are more familiar to many than we would like. With so many forces in place against the survival of the family, should people not be eager to do whatever they can to strengthen it?

GOD'S BLUEPRINT

A lot of residential building is going on today in Houston, Texas. New areas are developed constantly, and older neighborhoods seem virtually reborn overnight as smaller, older homes are torn down to make room for larger, more modern ones. And the way houses are built today is different from what I recall. I was at a construction site recently and noticed that I didn't see any hammers. I was astounded. But hammers are apparently passe. Nails are now "shot" from guns with one lick. No pounding involved—just aim and fire. A man I know who is in the building business told me he was on a job site a while back and no one could locate a hand saw! Imagine—builders with no saw!

We have learned a great deal about building houses. They seem to go up overnight, and they are lovely, well-built things. But how little has been learned about building homes. And how few real homes are in existence today, even within the Christian community. How few begin with a dynamic, exciting, Christ-centered relationship between husband and wife built on God's principles and lived by His grace.

When God created man, he created them male and female. He saw that it was not good for the man Adam to be alone, so he made a helper for him. There was tremendous potential for oneness, and the miraculous capacity to reproduce life. This was the first sociological unit in the world—the family. God in his wisdom knew that the basic foundation of society would be the home, the family, and He gave clear instruction—first through speech and then through His Word—as to how this unit should operate. Through the pages of the Bible, He still speaks about how the family is to work—how a husband is to relate to his wife, a wife to her husband, and children to their parents. There is no guesswork. No one has to throw up his arms and say, "I have no idea how this whole thing is supposed to look!"

> *God in His wisdom knew that the basic foundation of society would be the home, and He gave instruction as to how this unit should operate.*

The essential information is there but has not been used. Behind beautiful houses today, there are very few homes. Former Education Secretary William J. Bennett said as much in a recent report issued by the Hudson Institute entitled "Index of Leading Cultural Indicators." In it he wrote that since 1960 "there has been a 500 percent increase in violent crime; more than a 400 percent increase in illegitimate births; a quadrupling of divorce rates; a tripling of the percentage of children living in single-parent homes; more than a 200 percent increase in the teenage suicide rate; and a drop of almost 80 points in the SAT (college aptitude test) scores."[1]

The April 1993 issue of *Atlantic* magazine devoted almost half of its pages to the troubled American family, and its cover trumpets that fact with these words:

DAN QUAYLE WAS RIGHT. After decades of public dispute about so-called family diversity, the evidence from social-science research is coming in: The dissolution of two-parent families, though it may benefit the adults involved, is harmful to many children, and dramatically undermines our society."[2]

Everyone has basic needs. And God designed the home to be the primary place where those needs are met. Some have said the home is like a restaurant where people are "fed" with love. Others liken the home to a motel—mostly a place for spending the night, but not where real living takes place,

> *Everyone has basic needs. And God designed the home to be the primary place where those needs are met.*

and sadly that is sometimes true. Or the home has been compared to a bank where there is borrowing and lending and negotiation. That's not a bad picture. But the best analogy I have heard compares the home to a full-service filling station. That's something I know about.

When I was growing up, my dad had a country store. Next to that store he built a little building to use as a filling station with tanks out front. It was never really operational until the summer he said, "Edwin, I want you to go out and run the filling station." It sat about 20 yards from the main store—just far enough for a man to be an independent operator, and just close enough to shout for help! So that summer, I became a small businessman. I was fired up. Every morning for three months, I got up, put on my attendant's uniform (white tee shirt, Keds tennis shoes, and blue jeans) and went to work.

My dad taught me a few things about the business before he turned it over to me. "First," he said, "when a car pulls up, say 'fill 'er up?'" A lot of folks back in those days bought a dollar's worth of gas, and they were proud to get it. But "fill 'er up" Dad said was a positive word—so it was my first greeting, every day.

"Then," he said, "check under the hood. Wash off all the windows." I'll tell you; I could wash windows on a car quicker than anybody you have ever seen, because when you worked for my dad you did it right! So I'd put in the gas, I'd wipe off the windows, and I'd check the tires. Then I'd say, "Need that oil changed?" I was trying to see if they needed anything other than gasoline. I was taking care of the customers who came to our little full-service filling station.

And I think the home should be just like that. Do you know why? Because it is a tough, tough world out there. Husbands know that when they leave home in the morning, they enter a world that is basically godless. Wives who work know this too. The air is filled with profanity, vulgarity, and lewdness. It is dog-eat-dog. It is get-and-grasp. It is lying and deception. Fraud. Pushing. Undercutting. Most people work in a jungle.

For wives whose work is primarily in the home, the pressures, while different, are equally draining. Preparing children for school. Planning meals. Shopping. Cleaning. Carpooling. Children go off to school, where they face unbelievable pressures, much sooner than parents would imagine or would like to believe.

> *Cars converge on the full-service filling station called the home. Who is going to put on the attendant's uniform, rush out, and say "fill 'er up?"*

Toward the end of each afternoon, the family begins to converge on the home. Moms and dads wind up another day of work. Children return home from school. Dad's tank is empty. He has been roughed up by the world all day, and he is tired, disheartened, frustrated. Mom has been pulled in six-teen different directions since about 6:00 a.m. She's beat. Her tank is empty. The children return home all out of love. They're empty.

Cars converge on the full-service filling station called the home. Who is going to put on the attendant's uniform, rush out, and say "fill 'er up"? Who is going to do it? Everyone is empty. Is it Dad's job? Does he not deserve to sit and watch the news and wait for his dinner? Is it Mom's job? That does not seem fair. So much is expected of wives and mothers in our society. Is it the children's responsibility? Are they not pressured enough? Who puts on the white tee shirt, jeans, and tennis shoes and comes to fill the tank? Everybody! It is everybody's job. You see, each one is to be customer AND attendant in his home.

The outside world is tough, and that fact will never change. The real tragedy is that many homes are tougher still. Home should be a place to meet one another's needs for affection, sexual fulfillment, inti-mate communication, and companionship. When this is done, the home will become a place of romance—and will be associated with pleasure and security and fun. Each member will be filled and strengthened by mo-ments there and better equipped to face the world beyond its doors.

The Bible tells us that "God so loved the world that He *gave* His only begotten Son . . . " so that you might have eternal life—and so that those who are takers might learn to become givers. That, too, is part of salvation—to become like the Savior who was the ultimate giver. The ideal marriage is not give and take. It is give and give.

So how do you do it? How do you imitate Jesus Christ in this broken world and learn to fill one another? I believe there are three simple things that are incredibly **A LOOK, A WORD, A TOUCH** filling to any husband, wife, or child. They are not particularly complicated or artistic like a chocolate souffle—they are more like bread: warm, simple, and satisfying. Three things: a look, a word, a touch.

Two years ago I was in Dallas, Texas, at a basketball game for high school All-Stars. My youngest son Cliff and another young man from his high school were competing with athletes from private schools across the state. As I said before, I have been to hundreds of basketball games with our boys—and I have loved every one of them. It is a good thing they do not schedule games at 9:40 or 11:00 a.m. on Sunday mornings or our pulpit would be empty, because my priorities are God first, family second, and vocation third.

At the end of this particular game, the floor was full of people, and in the midst of the confusion, I saw Cliff look up at me in the stands—just a long, long look at his dad. And that look of love just filled my tank! That is all it took. Just a moment, just a look, and I was full. You can love someone, believe in them, think they are great, but unless you express that with a word, a look, or a touch, they may never know it.

A young woman in our church family recalls that when she turned thirteen, she received a letter, written by her dad, in which he remembered significant events in her young life, and tried to say in words all that she meant to him and her mother. It was accompanied by a single red rose. She is in her thirties today and the rose has long since faded, but she still has the letter tucked away, and reads it every now and then—and she is filled, every time.

Every once in a while, I have a special date with a great gal who is not my wife. Her name is Lee Beth, and she is my six-year-old granddaughter. One Friday night I picked her up—just the two of us—to go and do something fun together. She was so dressed up, and I put her in the car and buckled her seat belt. Then I asked her where she wanted to go, and she named about five restaurants, emphasizing McDonald's, but agreeing to Chick Fil-A since it was in the mall.

We went to the shopping mall and had one of those chicken sandwiches together. We held hands the whole time. Then we did a little shopping, and I bought her a pair of pink shoes. (They ended up being too large, but her mom said she would grow into them by Easter.) Finally we walked out to the car to go home, and I was so excited about the date that I forgot where I had parked. But that was okay, because she helped me find the spot, and we got to walk around together and hold hands a little longer. Then we got home and she looked at me and said, "I love you, Goosie," and I tell you—between the looks and her touch and those words—I was filled to overflowing. Do you see how it works?

Where did those looks and those words and that touch come from? We made time to do something together, she and I. When you spend fun time with your mates and loved ones, you set the stage for intimacy. When a husband and wife do this, they discover the joy of being not just lovers—but friends. "This is my beloved," the bride said in the Song of Solomon, "and this is my friend."

Conscientously seek to meet the needs of your mate. When you do, no matter what the state of your house, the home inside will be rich and warm and strong.

Will you "Fill 'er up"?

1. What was the last "recreational" outing that you and your mate took? Who initiated it? Who enjoyed it the most? Do you plan to do it again? Why or why not?
2. Make a list of recreational pursuits that you enjoy, and ask your mate to do the same. Compare your lists to see if there are any common themes, then make a date with one another to enjoy them together.

QUESTIONS FOR FURTHER REFLECTION

3. What does your mate absolutely love to do that you have no interest in? Have you tried it? Can you "go along" cheerfully, even if you don't participate? Are you willing to?

4. Each day, determine to fill your mate with either a look, a word, a touch—or a combination of all three. Find a way to communicate each day "I like being with you."

10

You Look
Marvelous!

*A Husband Needs:
An Attractive Wife*

THE APOSTLE PETER HAD A GREAT
deal to say about attractiveness:

> In the same way, you wives, be submissive to your own
> husbands so that even if any of them are disobedient
> to the word, they may be won without a word by the
> behavior of their wives, as they observe your chaste and
> respectful behavior. And let not your adornment be
> merely external—braiding the hair, and wearing gold
> jewelry or putting on dresses; but let it be the hidden
> person of the heart, with the imperishable quality of a
> gentle and quiet spirit, which is precious in the sight
> of God. For in this way in former times the holy
> women also, who hoped in God, used to adorn them-
> selves, being submissive to their own husbands. Thus
> Sarah obeyed Abraham, calling him lord, and you have

become her children if you do what is right without being frightened by any fear (1 Pet. 3:1-6).

In an ancient Greek myth a king named Pygmalion searched long and hard for the woman of his dreams, but to no avail. He knew the kind of woman he wanted for a wife, but he just couldn't seem to find her. When his frustration reached its peak, he came to what seemed a very sensible solution.

If the woman of his dreams did not exist, he would create her himself! Since Pygmalion was a sculptor, he used the tools of his trade to fashion a beautiful woman out of the finest ivory. When he was done, he bowed before his creation and prayed, and the woman came to life! She was, in the flesh, what his heart had longed for, and he wasted no time in making her his wife.

It is a beautiful story, is it not? Who has not longed for a perfect mate—made to order just for us? Eventually people meet and marry the one closest to that ideal.

Someone once said that women often marry thinking they will change their mate, and men marry thinking their mate will never change! I think that is pretty accurate.

A modern version of Pygmalion's search culminated recently when Japan's Crown Prince Naruhito announced he had found the woman of *his* dreams. His criteria were reported worldwide just two years ago.

The prince wanted an intelligent, attractive, athletic and discreet young Japanese woman from a leading business, diplomatic or academic family with no previous boyfriends. She had to be fluent in English and also, ideally, French; had to be no taller in heels than 5'4," no older than 25; be prepared to give up considerable freedom in exchange for ladies in waiting, overseas travel, and opportunities to meet world leaders. He would accept independent-minded career women, but no daughters of politicians.

Employing patience and diligence, he apparently came very close to his ideal mate. She is extremely intelligent and attractive and from an excellent family. She is multi-lingual and well-educated. She is the right height. She is slightly older than his upper limit of 25—but so far, no ex-boyfriends have surfaced. She fits the bill almost to a "t."

Did you happen to notice the second thing on Prince Naruhito's wish list? He wanted an attractive wife. Is anyone surprised? I think it is safe to say that every man desires an attractive wife. Dr. Harley's survey indicates an attractive wife is "number 3" on a list of the top five needs of husbands. Before we explore this need further, I believe we would be wise to define *attractive*. The dictionary defines an attractive person as someone who is "pleasing or handsome." That is great as far as it goes, but it does not go quite far enough. What is pleasing or handsome? Who decides on the standard?

What was considered beautiful or attractive one hundred years ago would seem strange by contemporary standards. The female standard of attractiveness was once a very Rubenesque figure, demonstrated in Renaissance painting and sculpting. A little over two decades ago a British fashion model named Twiggy was considered the female ideal. Twiggy weighed less than one hundred pounds and her measurements sounded more like those of a malnourished child than a high-fashion model. Today muscles are in for females—and a lean, muscled woman is considered by many to be highly attractive. These social standards of attractiveness are constantly changing, however, with different physical characteristics coming in and out of fashion.

Most women are much more concerned with being thought of as attractive by the one that they love than they are with measuring up to shifting cultural trends. Whoever said "beauty is in the eye of the beholder" was much closer to the truth of what is attractive. God provides in His Word an even better (and constant) picture of what is attractive in a woman, and it goes far beyond physical appearance.

> In the same way, you wives, be submissive to your own husbands so that even if any of them are disobedient to the word, they may be won without a word by the *behavior* of their wives, as they observe your chaste and respectful behavior (1 Pet. 3:1-2).

Pretty Is as Pretty Does The first thing that makes a woman attractive, Peter says, is her behavior. She should be chaste and respectful, he wrote, and submissive to her husband. Some wives might say, "Hey, wait a minute. If I had the right kind of man I would be chaste and respectful. But I don't have that kind of man." These verses were written just for those women—women who have exactly the wrong kind of man. This word is for the woman married to a man who is godless and cold and calculating. And Peter said the wife of such a man is to live before him with the kind of behavior that will make him want to get his life right with God.

I have met a lot of different people in my 30-plus years of work. I have met athletes and movie stars, presidents and senators, authors, speakers, astronauts and others. Two women that I have met come immediately to mind when I think of what is attractive and what is not. One is a leading sex symbol of our time. I

The best advice Peter could offer this kind of woman was not "work hard and change your man." It was "make your behavior so attractive that your man will do the changing himself." He may have rejected the Word, but it is hard to deny the presence of a life that is a living sermon. An attractive wife, a wife that is pleasing to her husband, is radiant in her love for God and consistent in her devotion to Him and to her husband.

will not give her name, but she is known by millions. The other is a former Miss America and many would know her name as well. These two women are beautiful by the world's standards. I spoke to each of them for over an hour, and nothing that was said indicated that either had any reverence for or knowledge of God whatsoever. They were grasping, cold, tough-minded, obnoxious women—both of them!

If you saw either of them on the street, you might be tempted to say they were the most attractive women you had ever seen. But I am convinced that if you spent time with them, you would certainly change your mind. Externally, by the world's standards, they are "knockouts." Internally, they are hollow. Behavior is a key component of attractiveness. My mother was right about this one: pretty *is* as pretty does.

Here's Looking at You

An attractive wife behaves in a chaste and respectful manner. But attractiveness is a function of appearance, as well:

> And let not your adornment be merely external— braiding the hair and wearing gold jewelry, or putting on dresses. (1 Pet. 3:3)

I can remember preachers from my boyhood in Mississippi who would take this passage as a proof text that ladies should never go to the beauty parlor or wear jewelry, but I never heard a single one say that women should stop putting on dresses! But Peter simply said that if a woman goes to the trouble of adorning the outside, she should not stop there! He took for granted that women will strive to do the best they possibly can with what God has given them. They will braid their hair. They will wear accessories. They will wear dresses. And he did not recommend otherwise. He said that appearance is an important aspect of attractiveness, although by no means is it the only one.

This may be a dangerous thing for me to say, but apart from medical or physiological conditions (and there are very few of them) that are beyond a person's control, I believe men and women alike should be able to keep their bodies in good shape. I believe God calls us to do so since the body is the temple of the Holy Spirit, and the very place where Jesus Christ dwells. Paul wrote to the church at Rome:

> I urge you therefore, bretheren, by the mercies of God, to present your bodies a living and holy sacrifice, acceptable to God, which is your spiritual service of worship (Rom. 12:1).

I am constantly amazed at what a volatile topic this is! If reading that you are to glorify God and please your mate by keeping your body in shape angers you, good! The Bible says more about the sin of gluttony than it does about any of the other seven deadly sins. At its root, gluttony is a desire to fill some inner emptiness. Peter Kreeft, in his book *Back to Virtue,* explains:

> The motivation for gluttony is the unconscious self-image of emptiness: I must fill myself because I am empty, ghost-like, worthless. Only a knowledge of God's love for me can fill that emptiness, make me a solid self, give me ultimate worth. And that knowledge comes through Jesus Christ. Therefore Jesus is the ultimate answer to gluttony, as to every other one of our problems. "My God shall supply all your needs . . . by Christ Jesus," Saint Paul assures us.[1]

For a wife to be physically attractive, she must work at keeping her body in shape. If you are overweight, the answer is not a crash diet or some bizarre and difficult-to-adhere-to eating plan. Being in shape is a simple matter of mathematics. Balance calorie intake with the amount of energy expended in exercise and daily living. In most cases, it is that simple. If you take in more calories than your body burns, over time you will gain weight, and the excess will go to fat. To maintain weight, eat sensibly and engage in some aerobic form of exercise (aerobic activity uses 60 to 70 percent of the heart's maximum capacity) at least three times a week.

My friend and fellow jogger, Dr. George Boutros, says that to lose weight, you must exercise four to five times per week and maintain the same caloric intake. Some excellent books on the market explain this in greater detail, but simply and plainly, it is a matter of balancing what is consumed with what is spent.

When someone looks better, they feel better about themselves. An attractive wife works at her appearance. She cares about her hair. She takes an interest in how she looks to her husband. She continues to put her best foot forward and to make the most of the unique beauty God has given her.

A husband sees in his wife something he saw in no one else. He married her. When she is pleased with her appearance, he is pleased as well. Peter says an attractive wife behaves in a chaste and reverent way, and that her appearance is not *just* external—but the external is well-cared for, too. When a woman takes pride in her appearance and takes care to look her best, her husband is proud of her too. Even when she is 90 years old, a wise wife remembers that she needs to be some facsimile, regardless of age and the toll of time, of what she was when her husband fell in love with her.

Peter also spoke of another equally important aspect of a wife's attractiveness in 1 Peter 3:4:

BEAUTY OF THE SPIRIT

> But let it be the hidden person of the heart, with the imperishable quality of a gentle and quiet spirit, which is precious in the sight of God.

Physical beauty may certainly fade with time, but there is a beauty that will never fade, and that is a gentle and quiet spirit. I do not believe the apostle wrote about whether a woman is an introvert or an extrovert, or whether she is loud or soft-spoken. I believe he focused on the kind of spirit that says a woman has dignity. This quality will not perish, nor will it dim with time. Instead, it will be enhanced with age, with maturity, with love, and with care.

How does a woman get that imperishable quality of a gentle and quiet spirit? It comes from knowing God— and from cultivating a relationship with Him that is fed by His Word and nurtured by time spent with Him. It comes when she employs the spiritual disciplines of prayer, silence, and meditation. But understand that when anyone makes the decision to know more of God, their fleshly nature will fight with that desire. A woman who wants to build within her life the character of the Lord, to become beautiful inside, can take comfort in the words of God spoken through the prophet Isaiah:

> My thoughts are not your thoughts, neither are your ways My ways, declares the Lord. For as the heavens are higher than the earth, so are My ways higher than your ways and My thoughts than your thoughts (Isa. 55:8-9).

When you begin to know His thoughts and His ways, God begins to change you and to build the right stuff into your life. The metamorphosis is radical and compelling. But to get there takes times of solitude, of quiet and holy reverence. These verses describe how an attractive woman behaves and how she appears, but Peter went a step further to give an example of the kind of woman he was describing:

> For in this way in former times the holy women also, who hoped in God, used to adorn themselves, being submissive to their own husbands. Thus Sarah *obeyed* Abraham, calling him lord, and you have become her

children if you do what is right without being frightened by any fear (1 Pet. 3:5-6, italics added).

I realize I will not win any popularity contests by saying that part of Sarah's beauty was that she obeyed her husband Abraham. But the word *obey* here is not a bad one; it simply means "to pay close attention to." Sarah paid close attention to Abraham, and she is Peter's example of an attractive, godly woman and wife. Sarah's relationship with Abraham would benefit any marriage; she simply paid attention to the man she married. She studied him. She knew his likes, his dislikes, his "triggers," his moods.

Wives today have a great temptation to get involved in many good causes, charity events, activities and hobbies. There are so many things to do, and so much of it is worthwhile. But if God has called you to marriage, few things are more important than your husband or your family. They deserve your best, not just what is left of you when everything else has been accomplished.

Can you imagine Abraham coming in from a long day of sheep herding? He is exhausted. He has been up since before daylight. He is dangerously hungry and sniffs the air hopefully as he approaches the tent that he and Sarah share, wondering what might be cooking for their dinner. As he gets closer, he sees a note pinned to the tent flap, and his heart sinks as he reads:

Abe, I've gone to a meeting with the Bethel ladies. Will be home late. Took small chariot. The mutton casserole in the stone furnace is for dinner. Don't worry—it's already cooked. Please remember to give Ishmael his herb cough juice, and Isaac desperately needs a bath! Love, Sarah. P.S. Close the flaps on the tent—I hear there's a sandstorm coming through tonight.

Can you imagine it? Not from Sarah, perhaps. But today? Wives, pay close attention to your husbands. If you do not, you are missing out on being the kind of wife that God wants you to be.

A little five-year-old girl came home from kindergarten. She had heard the story of Prince Charming and Snow White for the first time, and she was anxious to tell it to her mother. "Prince Charming came in on a white horse," she said, "and he got down off the horse, and he kissed Snow White, and she came back to life. And do you know what happened then?" she asked her mother. Her mother said, "Yes, I do. Then they lived happily ever after."

"Oh, no," the little girl said. "Then they got married!" That was a smart little girl. Marriage cannot necessarily be equated with living happily ever after. But wives, understanding that your husband wants an attractive wife can help you to equate the two. And, husbands, there is something you can do to help.

A Ten-Cow Wife Johnny Lingo lived many years ago on the island of Oahu, Hawaii. He was known as a trader, a man who could get anything for you at a price lower than anyone else could manage. He was smart and cagey, and he could negotiate better than any man on the island. This ability had made him very rich and equally well-respected.

It was the custom at this time for men to offer the fathers of their prospective wives a certain number of cows in exchange for their daughters' hand in marriage. The standard price was three cows, and most deals were struck for that price. Every once in a great while a girl would go for four cows, but she would be exceptionally beautiful and very much in demand. There was even an unsubstantiated rumor that a young girl with truly beautiful features, great charm, and strong character had gone for five cows, but no one could remember her name or the details of the match.

One man on the island lived with his two daughters. The younger one was very pretty and desirable. She was at least a three-cow bride, perhaps four. Her older sister, still unmarried, was not very attractive at all, and her father had little hope of getting even two cows for her. He had decided some time before that if a suitor came who offered one cow, he would let her be taken for that, but no one came to call.

One day, Johnny Lingo came to this man's house. Everyone assumed he was calling for the younger girl, and people began to speculate. The girl was ravishing, but no one could bargain like Johnny Lingo. Who would come out on top—Johnny, or the girl's father? Would Johnny hold out for a low price of three cows? Would her father insist on no less than four? Everyone on the island was breathless in anticipation of the negotiations.

Then something very strange happened. Johnny Lingo asked to see the older daughter! Her father was dumbfounded. He thought perhaps he had misunderstood. Surely Johnny meant his younger daughter? "No," Johnny said. "The older." He would not be swayed. The old man was beside himself with joy! His worst fear was that he would be forced to give the girl away, but now the richest man on the island was inquiring about her. Everyone knew that Johnny was as generous as he was rich, and they began to speculate about the price he would give for this homely daughter. Surely he would pay at least the standard three-cow price! Then again, maybe just to make a point, he would offer four cows. Or perhaps, just to say that no one had paid more for a wife than Johnny Lingo, he would offer five cows!

Can you imagine the shock when hard-bargaining Johnny Lingo offered ten cows for the least-desirable girl on the island? Her father was beside himself. He quickly agreed and hastily arranged the marriage, fearing that Johnny would realize the extravagance of his offer and back out of the deal. Johnny had no such intent. He just smiled, paid the ten cows, and announced that he and his ten-cow wife were going on a two-year honeymoon and would return after that to make their home on the island. Two years passed, and then a lookout was posted to search the horizon for the returning bride and groom. He spotted Johnny easily—everyone knew Johnny—but he wasn't sure that this was the same woman he had left the island with. She was vaguely familiar, but so incredibly beautiful that it was hard to believe she was the one.

She walked with confidence; she was gracious and self-assured. And when the town gathered around them, all who were there agreed that the change in Johnny's bride was unbelievable. Those who had laughed for months over the price he paid were now saying what a bargain he had gotten! Many agreed they would have paid twenty cows for a woman this attractive.[2]

What happened? What changed this woman from an unattractive wallflower to a compelling, vital, beautiful ten-cow bride? The same thing that happens today when a man treats his wife as the woman he desires her to be. Goethe has said, "If you treat a man as he is, he will stay as he is. If you treat him as if he were bigger than he ought to be, he will become that bigger and better man." The same is true of any woman alive. Husbands, do you want an attractive wife? Let her know that she is beautiful in your eyes and watch her blossom into the beauty that God created her to be!

I read once that when a pretty woman goes by, teenaged boys turn their heads and look. When a beautiful woman goes by, grown men turn their heads and look. When a gorgeous woman walks by, her husband turns his head and looks. I married a gorgeous woman. An attractive woman is appealing first and foremost to her husband. Her behavior is attractive. Her appearance is attractive. And her character is attractive.

God's Word is a mirror that can tell a woman how she really appears. Turn to the book of James, chapter 1, and look in the mirror. And with your eyes on God's Word, wives, say "I am going to seek as never before to be an attractive wife—a godly wife." When you do, you will begin to see that "married" and "happily ever after" just might be the same thing, after all.

Questions for Further Reflection

1. Do you agree or disagree with the saying "Pretty is as pretty does"? Husband, what things does your wife do that make her beautiful to you? Tell her about them.
2. The Bible tells us to make our bodies a living and holy sacrifice to God and to glorify God in our bodies. What does that mean? How would serious obedience to those directives change your personal habits?
3. Wife, are you cultivating a relationship with God that nurtures "the imperishable quality of a gentle and quiet spirit"? If not, how could you begin to do so?

11

THERE'S NO PLACE LIKE HOME

A Wife Needs: A Family Man
A Husband Needs: Domestic Support

WHEN GEORGE AND BARBARA BUSH resided at the White House, their bedroom rivaled the "situation room" or any east- or west-wing office for activity in the early morning hours. The Bushes made no apology for the fact that they liked to "bunk in" in the early morning hours, reading, watching the news, catching up on talk, and, when their extended family was in town, playing with "the grands." For the Bushes, the bedroom replaced the living room, the kitchen, and the den as a center of family activity.

This is true in our home as well. Our king-size bed is a gathering place where our boys have talked and played through the years. Jo Beth and I watch television, read, study, snack, and do crossword puzzles there—and every Saturday night I sit at the side of our bed in a little chair and study my sermon until very early the next morning. I thought perhaps this was a phenomenon limited to the White House and our house, until I read a feature article in a national paper some time back describing how the bedroom has become the new center of family life.

There is even a group called the Bed, Bath and Linen Association whose president says that the reason this room has become a focal point for families in the nineties is that we are all exhausted from the frenzied pace of the eighties. For this reason, we need a safe place—a cocoon—to protect us from the world outside and its harsh demands. This group contends that the "cocooning instinct" is what makes baby boomers "bunk down" in the security and safety of their homes, eschewing social commitments, entertaining, and endless attempts to "network."

> *We need a safe place—a cocoon—to protect us from the world outside and its harsh demands.*

HOME SWEET CASTLE

This book began by likening marriage to a private castle—a place where husband and wife would be safe and sheltered from the storms of living. Such a shelter sounds inviting, especially to a man. While bachelors, most men seem uninterested in domestic things. A bachelor is a man with a TV dinner in one hand and a remote control in the other. Laundry is at best a confusing prospect and at worst an excuse to buy new clothes. Some men have an interest in decorating the place where they live, but others report their most tired belongings mysteriously lost soon after they marry. In spite of their unstudied approach to domesticity in bachelor days, men enter marriage with a strong desire (often unexpressed) to "bunk down" in the kind of home that bears a woman's touch.

A contemporary male fantasy of hearth and home might go something like this: He hits the door at 6:00 p.m. or so, looking a little worse for the wear. Before he opens it, he can identify the smell of his favorite dinner cooking. There are no children screaming, dogs and cats chasing one another or toys scattered pell-mell in the yard and on the porch. As he enters, he hears the melodious voice of his beautiful wife call out from another room: "Hi, darling. I'm so glad you're home. How was your day?"

He stumbles to the den, drops his coat and paper, and pulls off his shoes. His wife appears and gives him a hug and a kiss. There is a fire in the fireplace, crackling nicely, and giving the room a golden glow. She snuggles down next to him and describes in mouth-watering detail the meal that will be ready soon. Soft music plays somewhere in the house, and in a few minutes the children come in, hug their dad, then go back to their homework until time for dinner.

After a relaxing and delicious meal together, the children clear off the table while husband and wife linger. Homework is finished and the kids come back in to watch television for a short while. He finishes the paper, drinks a cup of hot tea with honey, then together they put the children to bed. Prayers are said, hugs and kisses are dispensed, and then there are a few quiet moments alone before going to bed together at a reasonable hour.

Is this a rerun of the "Dick Van Dyke Show"? No! It is a rerun of what many men imagine when they picture a home and marriage. Is it realistic? Probably not, but that does not change the fact that men have a strong desire for the kind of domestic tranquility it represents. "But this is the nineties," someone will argue. "No one lives like that anymore, if they ever did." Oh, but men still dream.

In contrast to a man's dream of domestic harmony, there is the reality of daily living. Real life goes more like this: He trudges in at 7:30 after a late meeting. He is starved, but she has had to feed the kids and put his dinner in the refrigerator. "Call Domino's if you don't want it," she suggests. There is a squabble over a Nintendo game going on down the hall that sounds as if it might require military intervention. The dog has wet on the carpet. Again. The phone rings, and it is his mother. She puts him on the phone, even though he has motioned that he is not officially home yet.

After a half-hour conversation on caladiums and tulip bulbs, he decides to forego dinner, noticing that a basketball play-off game is on cable. As he reaches for the remote control, his youngest daughter comes in and announces she must watch a special on butterfly migration for extra credit in life science. She needs the credit, so he hands over the remote. He pats the sofa next to him and motions for his wife to sit down, thinking this might be a good time for a quiet talk. The dog jumps up next to him.

Everyone still needs a place to go when life is overwhelming . . . a hospital when hearts are broken.

She goes to their room and he hears the sound of the shower. When the butterfly special is over, he goes in to tell her that her favorite singer is on "The Tonight Show," but she has fallen asleep with the lights still on. He reads for a while, then tries not to wake her up as he climbs in bed exhausted. As he turns out the light he hears a small voice from down the hall: "Daddy, I don't feel good. I think I'm going to be sick." And so ends the fantasy of perfect domestic tranquility.

Everyone needs a place to go when life is overwhelming in the middle of the week. All need a "hospital" when their hearts are broken, a sane haven when they are psychologically frustrated. When people are upset and depressed and defeated, they still long for a place to retreat and be encouraged. And if given first choice, they would choose to receive those things at home. But what if the home is not functioning in this way? What if there is turmoil and conflict in the home, and it offers not solutions, but more problems? What then?

The one place that could be a shelter—a welcome haven—often represents just another series of items on our to-do lists. "Feed children." "Mow grass." "Repair kitchen sink." "Do grocery shopping." Instead of looking forward to going home at the end of a working day, some men and women avoid going home because they know that more demands await them there.

Each person has the same 24 hours in a day to work with. No one can get anymore than that. A good number of those waking hours are spent making a living since few are independently wealthy and can escape that requirement. If a husband and wife have children, a significant number of hours are spent caring for their needs. Then there are domestic responsibilities: meals, marketing, home maintenance, and repairs. The reality of making a home with someone is an enormous and time-consuming challenge.

Bars in my city and hundreds of others are filled with men and women each day during "happy hour." They are "happy" to be done with another day of work, and "happy" to have a place to go that requires little of them, except that they pay their bills before they leave. They flock to these establishments in droves, looking for someone to talk to, to share with, to commiserate with—things they evidently do not believe they would find at home.

Adults—husbands and wives—are not the only ones in a family that seek elsewhere what the home could offer. Children get battered and bruised by life, too, and they need some measure of domestic peace just to heal from the hurts of an ordinary day. I remember when I was in the third grade, a girl in my class named Carolyn had a birthday. My class was not that large—we all knew one another—and Carolyn lived right down the street, so I anticipated an invitation to her party. It never came. Everyone was invited to Carolyn's party, but not me. In fact, Carolyn said, "I didn't invite Edwin because I don't like Edwin." It does not get much clearer than that, does it? Over 40 years later, I still remember that hurt. Children's hurts are just as real as adults'.

> *With work and attention, we can make our marriages and homes a safe place to "bunk down" in the nineties.*

What happens when a child cannot go home and find love and acceptance—that safe "cocoon" of nurture? He turns to his peers for guidance and approval and is confronted daily with temptations to substitute alcohol, drugs, or sex for what he really wants and needs. But with work and attention, we can make our marriages and homes a safe place to "bunk down" in the nineties.

EDUCATION   Husbands and wives have no reason today to be ignorant about how they are to function in their marital roles. Too many books, videos, seminars, and articles abound for anyone to reasonably plead ignorance. Too many friends, family members, counselors, and pastors could help if someone admitted ignorance and sought to learn. I am not an accountant, but I understand that no one takes the CPA exam lightly. If you want to be a certified accountant, you study diligently to pass the exam. I know lots of lawyers, and not a single one has confided to me in the privacy of my study that they blew off the bar exam and just figured they would know the right answers intuitively. Physicians are rigorously tested to measure their competency before they practice and even afterwards must constantly study to keep up with the changes in their field.

> *Marriage is the most demanding and difficult "life" exam I know . . . To approach it with the idea that things will just work themselves out is naive.*

Marriage is the most demanding and difficult "life" exam I know. It also has the potential to be the most rewarding. But to approach it with nonchalance or the idea that things will just work themselves out is terribly naive. "Happy marriages, said Ruth Graham, wife of evangelist Billy Graham, "are never accidental. They are the result of good hard work." Part of that work is education about marital roles and parenting responsibilities. No one instinctively knows what to do.

When my oldest son Ed was in high school, he took a test on the amendments to the Constitution of the United States. Ed was oblivious to the finer points of civics at this point in his life. If he even knew we had a Constitution, I am sure it was news to him that there were amendments to it.

Knowing that he was studying for a test, I went to check on him. As I questioned him about what he was learning, he became more and more evasive. Sensing that we were in trouble, I picked up his textbook and asked him specific questions about the amendments. He did not know one from another.

I would like to report that I handled this beautifully, that I did what several leading experts would recommend in this parenting "test." But the truth is I failed. I went bonkers. I shouted. I lost my temper. I even think I said some "terminal words" like "If you can't learn the amendments to the Constitution, how are you ever going to amount to anything?" I stayed in his room until nearly 4 a.m. trying to drill the amendments into his memory, but I do not recall that he did very well on the test the next day. I should not have been surprised.

Today, I wish I had those words back. I needed to educate myself on motivating a teenager—and I learned at Ed's expense that shame and condemnation are not motivators. I acted out of ignorance. Parents need to be educated. Husbands and wives need to be educated if they are going to build the kind of cocoon that is desperately needed today in the lives of every member of their family.

OBSERVATION Not only do people need education, they need to sharpen their observation skills. My brother-in-law Joe Sanderson, is chairman of Sanderson Farms in Mississippi. On a visit to Houston, he and I went to a few grocery stores, and in each one he looked at how the chickens were packaged. He could tell me everything in the world about how those chickens were processed and prepared for sale: where they came from, how long they had been in the store, what quality they were. He is in the chicken business, so he observes.

Another man I know is in the roofing business. When I ride in the car with him, he notices roofs. "That's a cheap one," he might say. "It will be leaking in less than two years." He can tell this just by looking! He knows the material used. He knows how long each kind of roof will last. I am astounded at what he knows about roofs.

A man that I go fishing with can get out on a lake and know exactly where to cast his line. "Throw out over that way," he will say. "There ought to be fish over there." Sometimes I will say, "Why not over here?", indicating another spot. "Oh, no," he always insists, "that is not where the fish are going to be." And he is right nine times out of ten. It is amazing—but he observes.

How many would say that marriage is their business? That the family is their business?

I can walk onto a church campus or into a sanctuary and get a good idea of what is going on in the life of that church. It is my business, so I look, I listen, I observe. And I can tell you with pretty good accuracy whether that church is moving or standing still, whether or not people are coming to know Jesus Christ.

How many would say that marriage is their business? That the family is their business? I wonder how sensitive anyone really is to family life. Can you look at your mate and see quickly that something is just not right?

Are you that observant? Can you look at a child and see that something is amiss? Are you observant? Chickens and roofs and fish—even churches—will all pass away one day. But people are eternal, and there are no people you have more opportunity to observe and study than the ones that you live with.

Expression

All the education in the world and hours of observation are meaningless unless people put into practice what they learn. To do that requires expression, openness with mates and family members. I can come home all beat up from the pressures of the world, but unless I open up to my wife and my family, they cannot minister to me, and I cannot be bandaged up and helped. In the same way, if my wife or my children cannot communicate their real feelings to me, little healing will take place for anyone.

Usually men struggle more with this issue of expression. There is a rumor that it is not masculine for a man to let others really see his heart, expecially if it is broken. But that is not masculinity; it is pride and ego. People must open up and be real—at the very least to those that they live with.

This description by Evan S. Connell of a man bound by pride and fearful of expressing his heart is all too real:

> Often he thought: My life did not begin until I knew her. She would like to hear this, he was sure, but he did not know how to tell her . . . He needed to let her know how deeply he felt her presence while they were lying together during the night, as well as each morning when they awoke and in the evening when he came home. However, he could think of nothing appropriate.

> So the years passed, they had three children and accustomed themselves to a life together, and eventually Mr. Bridge decided that his wife should expect nothing

more of him. After all, he was an attorney rather than a poet; he could never pretend to be what he was not. [1]

A few years ago a man who was not a member of our church brought his son to participate in a week-long activity we sponsored for children. When he dropped him off on the second morning, he called a volunteer worker over to the side and said, "Bobby's not happy. I wonder if you could make him happy today?" The worker told this father that she had not noticed that Bobby was unhappy. In fact, she said he had interacted well with the other children, participating in all activities. Nevertheless, she and other workers watched Bobby closely all day. He seemed fine.

At the end of this day, the father came for Bobby and talked to him privately for a few minutes before approaching the same volunteer again. "Bobby's not happy," his father reported. "He just told me he wasn't happy. I want you to make him happy." The volunteer decided to ask Bobby and get the facts directly.

"Bobby," she said, "did you have a good time today?"

"Yes."

"Bobby, are you happy?"

He hesitated. "No," he finally responded.

"Well, then," she countered, "what would make you happy?"

"I want my Mommy and Daddy to live together again," he said.

As Bobby went off to the car, his father explained that he and Bobby's mother were divorced, that she lived up north, and that these few days of custody were his only contact with his son. The worker listened to all that he had to say, then responded: "I'm sorry that Bobby is unhappy. But we cannot provide here in this church all that your child needs. We can't be his home or his parents, and we can't change in a week what has happened over a period of years. We do the very best we can, but we can't do that. Bobby himself told you the one thing it would take to make him happy—and only you can provide it."

The father, broken now and just beginning to understand, said, "I'd give everything in my life to be able to go back and do it all over again." Then he started to say, "If only . . .," and the volunteer said a whole litany of "if only's" followed. If only I had done this. If only I had said that. If only I had known. If only I had observed. If only I had expressed my feeling. If only . . . if only . . . if only . . .

> *The church, the government, the schools will always be inadequate substitutes for a loving home that is a place of refuge and strength.*

All husbands, wives, and children need the security and peace that a home can provide. And the church, the government, the schools will always be inadequate substitutes for a loving home that is a place of refuge and strength. *Time* magazine, in a special issue entitled "Beyond the Year 2000: What to Expect in the New Millennium," predicted that the institution of the family and the traditional home will become relics unknown to future generations. A section dealing with marriage and parenthood carried the title "The Nuclear Family Goes Boom!," and called the idea that the family as we know it will not survive a reasonable one.

> Given the propensity for divorce, the growing number of adults who choose to remain single, the declining popularity of having children and the evaporation of the time families spend together, another way may eventually evolve. It may be quicker and more efficient to dispense with family-based reproduction. Society could then produce its future generations in institutions that might resemble state-sponsored baby hatcheries . . ."[2]

I've yet to meet a man who told me he longed deep in his heart for a "quicker and more efficient" way to exist and reproduce. What more men long for is a place to retreat from the demands of the world and *be*: be encouraged, be loved, be helped, be healed. I've had wives tell me the hardest words for their husbands to utter are the words "I love you," but I believe it is even harder for a man to say in all truthfulness "I need you" to his wife and his family. But we do. Oh, how we do.

Is There a Family Man Out There?

Wives also have a deep need related to the home. As much as a husband needs and desires a sense of domestic tranquility within his marriage, a wife needs and desires that her husband be a family man. Part of the security of the home to her is knowing that her husband is her number one fan in all of life, and that he is irrevocably committed to her and their family through the joys and sorrows it holds. A woman marries believing that the smallest drop of devotion that she sees is part of a rolling ocean—and too many men marry believing that the task of wooing and winning is now complete. Nothing could be further from the truth.

Every woman asks herself two questions in a dating relationship. The first is "What does he really want from me?," and the second is "How badly will I be hurt if he does not choose me?" A woman goes through the dance of courtship leaning away slightly, protecting herself until she is sure that she is truly loved and desired. A man, on the other hand, leans in slightly, pursuing. And he does all that he can to convince the woman he desires that he is worthy of her trust. She becomes his goal—and he places her in a position of utmost importance in his life to prove to her that she is important to him.

> *As much as a husband needs and desires a sense of domestic tranquility within his marriage, a wife needs and desires that her husband be a family man.*

Then the man and woman marry. She is preparing for a lifetime of "courtship devotion." He has achieved his goal of winning her and is ready to charge after his next goal. He thinks *The marriage thing is behind me. Super. Now I'm going on to my next task: to make my mark in the business world.* This is generally how men think, and they think this way because they are boys at heart. They make to-do lists and never think about the items on it once they are crossed off. Men tried out for sports teams, made the cut list, practiced, played the season, and then went on to the next thing. No looking back.

> *If a man wants his marriage to come alive and grow, he must continue to do all that he did to win his wife—and more.*

Women are not this way. A woman marries not thinking, *mission accomplished,* but, *if he was this attentive or kind or devoted in courtship, just think how wonderful it will be when we are married.* When the reality sets in, she feels deceived and cheated. The attention and sweetness of courtship are gone, because, well—this is marriage! But if a man wants his marriage to come alive and grow, he must continue to do all that he did to win his wife—and more. She needs to know that he is a family man—and that she and his children come first.

I believe men fail in this area for three reasons. First, some have not seen a good model of how to lead and love in the home. Perhaps their own fathers did not provide the example that they needed. Second, others have failed to lead because their wives would not allow it. Third, some are lazy and passive and unwilling to pay the price of being a family man.

While the price of being such a man is great, the destruction caused by falling short of it is even greater. The prophet Ezekiel illustrated this:

> Then the word of the LORD came to me saying, "What do you mean by using this proverb concerning the land of Israel saying, 'The fathers eat the sour grapes, but the children's teeth are set on edge'?" (Ezek. 18:1-2)

When the father eats sour grapes, the children's teeth are set on edge. If you've ever eaten a sour grape—or anything sour—you will remember that every past, present, and future cavity you have ever had came into play. These verses teach that when the father and husband goes astray—morally, biblically, or in whatever way—pain comes to the wife, certainly, but mostly to the children. Their teeth are set on edge.

Husbands and fathers should know that when they stand before God Almighty, He will make them account for the kind of family they have made. He will not ask the wife's sister or best friend if she did all that she could to make the wife the woman God called her to be. He will ask her husband. He will not call the babysitter, the daycare director, or the schoolteacher to inquire whether they nurtured and cared for and encouraged his children. He will ask their father. Men are accountable for loving their wives and caring for their children. No one else is. No one else.

A wonderful Christian family in Dallas lost their only son several years ago in a drowning accident. He was 24 years old and full of promise. Someone asked the father not long after the tragedy how he was able to cope with such a great loss. "I am able to handle it," he responded, "because as far as bringing up my son is concerned, my wife and I have no regrets. From the time he was born we poured all the energy and life and faith we had into that boy. We weren't perfect parents, but as we look at his developing years, we have no regrets."

I pray that as some are reading they will realize that they have not made the kind of home that God intended when their marriage began, and that they will ask for help. I pray that they will study and observe and express their thoughts and feelings in this all-important area. I hope that men commit to being the best husbands and fathers that they can be—and are willing to pay the price to make themselves "family men." And that in the years ahead, they too will be able to look at the homes they have made and say, "I haven't been perfect, but I have no regrets." Because there *is* no place under heaven like home.

1. Is your home a "safe place" to run to when the pressures of life prevail? Describe to your mate what you long for your home to be, and ask him or her to do likewise. What changes could be made to bring reality closer to your ideal?

2. Discuss Ruth Bell Graham's observation: "Happy marriages are never accidental. They are the result of good, hard work." Are you expecting your marriage to do what even your lawn cannot—to take care of itself?

3. Husband, do your wife and children come first with you? Do they know this?

4. Wife, is your husband your number one fan? Are you his most loyal supporter?

QUESTIONS FOR FURTHER REFLECTION

12

MONEY AND HOW IT MATTERS

A Wife Needs:
Financial Security

AMERICA IS OFTEN CALLED THE wealthiest nation in the world, yet in spite of its embarrassment of riches, Americans are trillions of dollars in debt. In 1960, 51 percent of Americans owed more than their net worth. Three decades later over 80 percent owed more than they owned. The percentage of people in this country who are financially secure is a very small one, even though the majority of our lifestyles demonstrate little evidence of want.

> *I believe that even today women desire financial security from the men that they marry.*

While it is not particularly popular to say so, I believe that even today women desire financial security from the men that they marry. They come to marriage with a need to be cared for in this way. I say this understanding that over half of the married women in America have careers outside the home. I realize that the two-career family is now considered the "norm" and that women have made tremendous strides in the areas of business, politics, law, and medicine. While it seems impossible today, just over 20 years ago women had difficulty signing a lease, obtaining a loan, or establishing credit without the cosignature of a man.

While times have changed, I am not at all sure that the needs of women have. One writer observes that what career women say about their working status and how they actually feel are often two different things:

> Whatever women say in public about their willingness to share the burden of making a living, in private I hear something entirely different. Married women tell me they resent working if their working is an absolute necessity. Even part-time work irritates them if their income has to help pay for basic living expenses.[1]

In fact, a recent Gallup poll indicates that half of all working couples with children would choose to have the mother stay at home full-time if money were not an issue.

Money—who makes it, how it is spent and by whom—is a sensitive marital issue. Some studies indicate that over half of all divorces take place over money matters. While I would disagree that money is the real problem, the undeniable fact is that checkbooks, credit cards, and past due bills are the feathers that fly in many disputes between husbands and wives. Perhaps the wedding vows should change to read "until debt do us part"—a more appropriate phrase for this generation caught up in a lust for things.

Meet Tom, for example. Tom is married to a lovely woman. They have a rather tight budget with limited assets, but whenever Tom goes out with the boys or he and his wife eat dinner out with other couples, he ignores that fact of life. He likes to be flamboyant and always insists on picking up the check. "You guys can't afford that," he says. "I'll take care of it. It's on me." That is Tom's nature and character. But when he gets home, his wife is incredulous: "Why do you insist on doing that when we struggle every month to make ends meet?" In public he is generous, but he pays the price for his generosity in private.

Then there is Dick. Dick and his wife both work, but Dick is not moving up the corporate ladder as quickly as either of them had hoped. Still, on his wife's birthday or other special occasions, he buys lavish, expensive gifts they cannot afford. His wife does not say anything, but her frustration grows when he buys things she does not want or need and they certainly can not justify based on their income. He is simply too extravagant and cannot seem to keep his gift-giving in line with their earnings.

Harry and his wife agreed early in their marriage that he would be the chief breadwinner. She would stay at home and he would provide financially for them both. But each month he gives her barely enough to make ends meet, and she has to justify how every cent of her "allowance" is spent. If she asks for anything extra, he explodes in a tirade that makes her feel so belittled she seldom bothers.

Alice is married and works outside the home. She and her husband determined that they would live off his salary and save hers, primarily for the down payment on a home and college expenses for their children. Sometimes Alice does put her earnings in savings, but more often than not she goes on spending binges, buying clothes, home furnishings—and whatever else is on sale. When her husband questions her actions she bristles, saying, "It's my money, and I can do with it what I want."

In each of these marriages, money is not a problem itself, but it may reveal another existing problem or harmful attitude. Consider family psychiatrist Samuel Pauker's observations:

> Money has enormous psychological significance for each of us. It is one of the primary ways we relate to others and think about ourselves. It represents a giving of ourselves and a taking from others. It is a "currency" of interpersonal negotiation. People often don't like to talk frankly about money and what it means to them, because they fear being considered rude or crude or greedy. But the fact is that money is so interwoven in the fabric of our lives that it inevitably becomes weighted with a myriad of meanings. It has to do with feeling taken care of or feeling cheated, feeling secure or insecure, feeling dependent or independent. Money often functions as a metaphor for a variety of other issues.[2]

Big spender Tom has an ego problem, revealed by his need to always pick up the tab, even when he's broke. Dick, who struggles in his vocation, is challenged by his wife who is successful in hers. So he tries to buy what he believes he has not been able to earn: her appreciation and trust and adoration. Harry uses money to dominate his wife and keep her "needy" before him by giving her just what she requires (and sometimes not even that) to pay the light bill and keep them in groceries. And Alice's separate bank account and runaway spending allow her to say in effect to her husband: "I can get what I want for myself without you." Money represents independence to her.

Or consider Bob and Mary. Soon after they were married they pursued their joint dream of a beautiful home. They called a real estate agent and house shopped on weekends. Before too long they found the dream home they had always wanted. The payments were a little more than they had planned to spend, but the neighborhood was perfect, so they took the plunge, with Mary promising to return to her former job to give them two incomes.

Anyone who is a homeowner understands that you do not just buy a home. You buy drapes and sprinkler systems and garage door openers and fences and gutters and . . . the list goes on. As the bills mounted, Bob took a second job, working most Saturdays to keep them afloat. Soon he spent little time in the home they had sacrificed to acquire—at least not waking hours. Then Mary discovered she was pregnant. They were thrilled. And they were terrified. He had two jobs. She was working overtime, expecting a child, and coming home exhausted day after day—until a week before the baby was born. Eighteen months later she was pregnant again, and this child had an unusual medical problem that meant more expenses. The dream that had seemed so bright just a few years before had become a trap they could not escape—no matter how hard they worked.

Does their story sound like make-believe? In place of Bob and Mary, I could fill in the names of scores of couples whose experience would verify its accuracy. This book is about romancing the home—building a marriage that sizzles and meeting one another's needs. A wife needs affection and communication. And she needs a sense of financial security from the man that she marries. Some men might say, "Well, my wife doesn't feel like that." Yes, she does. She just has not told you so. She does not want to marry a millionaire. She just needs to know that her husband (even if she works outside the home) is able and willing to care for her in this way. For most couples, the problem is not that they are unable to pay their bills, or that they are not working hard enough. The problem is mismanagement.

THE MONEY TRAP

A survey indicated that the average family felt that their financial difficulties could be solved with 25 percent more income. But when income increases, the wants seem to increase right along with it. Many people are surprised to learn that the Bible has something to say about this area of life. In fact, the Bible says more about money than it does about heaven or hell combined! This ancient book contains amazingly relevant principles regarding money management, stewardship, and budgeting.

> *The Bible says more about money than it does about heaven or hell combined, and contains amazingly relevant principles regarding money management, stewardship, and budgeting.*

> And while they were listening to these things, He went on to tell a parable, because He was near Jerusalem, and they supposed that the kingdom of God was going to appear immediately (Luke 19:11).

This particular parable is about Jesus' imminent departure and His coming again. It is prophetic in nature, but practical in its application. Jesus is the nobleman, and we are the servants or slaves left in charge of certain resources. And its message is relevant to assets, or money management.

> He said therefore, a certain nobleman went to a distant country to receive a kingdom for himself, and then return. And he called ten of his slaves, and gave them ten minas, and said to them, "Do business with this until I come back" (Luke 19:12-13).

The first lesson from this story is that God owns everything. It is not my part, your part, the bank's part, the government's part—it is all His. Every bit of what the Christian owns belongs to God. He owns everything.

This principle was vividly illustrated to me in McDonald's, of all places. I had gone to the home of the golden arches for lunch with my granddaughter, Lee Beth. We stood at the counter and placed our orders. She, with the confidence of youth and healthy arteries, ordered a "Happy Meal"—including a hamburger, French fries, and a drink. I, of the older and more "heart smart" generation, ordered a "McLean," with no fries. I paid for both of us, and we took our lunches to a nearby table and sat down. About halfway through our meal, I began to think how good one of Lee Beth's French fries would taste. It had been over a year since I had eaten a French fry, and I thought I might just help myself to one of hers. As I reached across the table she put her hand in front of mine and said with a stern warning, "No, Goosie, those are mine."

> *Every bit of what the Christian has belongs to God. He owns everything.*

But I bought every one of those French fries. And if I had wanted to, I could have marched back up to the counter and bought every other French fry in the house. As I thought about her response I began to understand how our childlike possessiveness of the things He provides must appear to God. He owns everything—and everything is at His disposal. Like the nobleman, He gives it to us to "do business with" for an undetermined time.

The ancient Hebrews had a view of life I believe we have lost today. They believed all of life was God's business. If you were a carpenter, you were an ordained carpenter—God's carpenter. If you were a fisherman, you were God's fisherman—and fishing was holy work.

Today, if you are a salesman, you can be God's salesman. If you are a doctor, you can practice medicine for God. Your work can be holy and as much an act of worship as a whispered prayer. But apparently workers in biblical times resented authority as much as some do today:

But his citizens hated him, and sent a delegation after him saying, "We do not want this man to reign over us" (Luke 19:14).

The inherent rebellion of man is captured in just these few words. We do not, at our very heart, want to be told what to do. Because the way God would do business is not always the way we would do business. These citizens did not want this nobleman to rule over them. They chafed under his authority. He gave them assets to "do business with," but they denied him a say in how those assets were used. Instead their attitude was "This is mine. I made it, I earned it, and I will do with it what I please." But a day of reckoning came.

> *There is no inherent virtue in poverty any more than there is inherent evil in wealth. Money is neutral.*

And it came about that when he returned, after receiving the kingdom, he ordered that these slaves, to whom he had given the money, be called to him in order that he might know what business they had done. And the first appeared, saying, "Master, your mina has made ten minas more." And he said to him "Well done, good slave, because you have been faithful in a very little thing, be in authority over ten cities." And the second came, saying, "Your mina, master, has made five minas." And he said to him also, "And you are to be over five cities" (Luke 19:15–19).

Is the nobleman displeased with profit? No! And God is not dishonored when people productively use the talents and abilities He has given them. There is no inherent virtue in poverty, any more than there is inherent evil in wealth. Money is neutral. The issue is not rich or poor, but rather how the "minas" God has given are used. Profit is okay; in fact, God requires it. He has invested a great deal in His people, and if they are not productive, they are the losers, and His kingdom suffers. Two of the men the nobleman entrusted made a profit—but a third did not.

> And another came, saying, "Master, behold your mina, which I kept put away in a handkerchief; for I was afraid of you, because you are an exacting man; you take up what you did not lay down, and reap what you did not sow." He said to him, "By your own words I will judge you, you worthless slave. Did you know that I am an exacting man, taking up what I did not lay down, and reaping what I did not sow? Then why did you not put the money in the bank, and having come, I would have collected it with interest?" And he said to the bystanders, "Take the minas away from him, and give it to the one who has the ten minas." (Luke 19:20-24)

It has been said that the rich get richer while the poor get poorer, and this story certainly bears that out. The man who made no use of what he was given had it taken away from him and given to the one who made the most! That offends the sense of fairness—just as it did the bystanders who heard the nobleman's words.

> And they said to him, "Master, he has ten minas already." "I tell you, that to everyone who has shall more be given, but from the one who does not have, even what he does have shall be taken away. (Luke 19:25-26)

John Wesley echoed the truths about money contained in this parable years later when he encouraged his followers to make all they could, save all they could, and give all they could. I believe this is sound advice. Make all you can! Save all you can! Give all you can! But make sure you do your giving in a way that will last forever.

I once had a bill with a one million mark on it—something few people have ever seen. It was the equivalent of 1,000,000 Argentinean pesos, and at one time (long before I owned it) it was worth hundreds of thousands of American dollars. It was given to me by a man who went to sleep one night and woke up the next morning to find that it was not worth the paper it was printed on. The currency standard changed literally overnight, and the money was worthless.

> *In God's economy, the real currency is what is given. God honors givers, not getters or keepers.*

The same thing is going to happen to each person one day. All will die—and all that they have worked for and slaved for and painstakingly collected is going to be worth zero. The only thing that will have worth then is what was invested in eternal causes—kingdom causes. And that will count for everything. Suppose Wall Street investors and stock market wizards said that all American currency would be invalid tomorrow—but that books would be our method of exchange. People would buy books! They would trade all that they could for books so that they could buy and sell tomorrow. In God's economy, the real "currency" is what is given. God honors givers, not getters, or keepers.

The book of Proverbs contains 36 different verses about how money is made, how it should be handled, and what it can and cannot do. John Wesley's advice was good: make all you can, save all you can, give all you can. I would add only one thing to it, and this is *borrow as little as you can.*

Paul wrote, "Owe nothing to anyone except to love one another" (Rom. 13:8), and some use his words as proof that Christians should never borrow. Only owing love is certainly an attractive ideal, but I have never known a lender due money to be satisfied with a note that read, "I sure do love you. Account paid in full!" A better translation of his instruction would be, "Don't keep on owing anyone." In other words, do not amass debt on top of debt. Keep short accounts. So make all you can, save all you can, give all you can, and borrow as little as you can.

HOW ABOUT A BUDGET?

I have never heard a financial expert recommend against establishing a budget. When they begin to record expenditures, most couples are astounded at where (and how quickly) their money is spent. Drawing up a budget can teach couples a great deal about how they view money, and requires them to establish joint financial goals at the outset. The budgeting process is the time to explore questions such as "How much income do we need to feel secure about our financial position?" "Is it generally more important to us to save for the future or to accumulate possessions?" "What sacrifices are we willing to make to achieve our stated goals?" "How will we pool our financial assets?" "Is it important for each of us to have some discretionary spending money, and if so, how much?"

As you answer these and other questions, you develop the basis for a workable financial plan. While you do so, take into account your present earnings and fixed expenses. If you work on a commission or salary-plus-commission or bonus basis, do not establish your budget based on the best month or year you've ever had. Be realistic.

And finally, determine as best you can the difference between your needs, your wants, and your desires.

People get into trouble with their finances because they are not able to discern between needs, wants, and desires. Each is distinctly different.

You may need water. You may want tea. You may desire Perrier. You may need hamburger. You may want a steak. But you may desire lobster. You may need a homemade dress, want a department store dress, and desire a designer dress. People get into trouble with their finances because they are not able to discern between needs, wants, and desires. They are distinctively different.

The apostle Paul demonstrated an understanding of this fact as he wrote to his younger brother in the faith, Timothy:

> For we have brought nothing into this world, so we cannot take anything out of it either. And if we have food and covering, with these we shall be content. But those who want to get rich fall into temptation and a snare and many foolish and harmful desires which plunge men into ruin and destruction. (1 Tim. 6:7-9)

Determine your needs, your wants, and your desires. To fail to understand the differences between them is to "fall into a temptation and a snare."

Most businesses are led by a board of directors. The board meets to set policy and outline the long-term direction of the company. They are the visionaries, the pacesetters of the operation, but their involvement is not usually hands on. The company's general manager or CEO translates those policies into operating procedures. He sees that the directors' priorities are carried out in the day-to-day operation of the company. The "buck" of financial accountability and decision making stops at his desk. But he seldom purchases a single thing on the company's behalf. A purchasing agent or vice president does that. Then an accountant or bookkeeper keeps the numbers straight. A payroll clerk sees that those who work for the company are regularly and fairly compensated.

I understand the limitations of equating the running of a business with the management of a family's finances, but there are definite similarities. The husband and wife—the board of directors—set the direction of this joint enterprise of marriage. One of them—frequently the husband, but certainly not always—translates those goals into operating procedures. Someone, too, must make actual purchases in line with those goals. This can be done jointly, but often this becomes the domain of the wife. Whoever is most skilled in the area of accounting generally inherits the bookkeeper function. And wise couples include training as well— teaching their children the mechanics of good financial management so that they, too, can participate.

More money management plans are available today than could ever be examined, but one that I have found particularly useful (and simple) is put forth by Dr. George Bowen in his book, *How to Be Successful With Your Money.* Dr. Bowen's recommendation is called the ten-seventy-twenty plan, and it is applicable to most situations, except perhaps very low or very high incomes which are more complicated. He suggests that couples consider Christ's admonition to render to Caesar that which is Caesar's and to God that which is God's first, by subtracting their taxes and their tithe from their gross monthly income. With the remainder, allocate 10 percent to savings, 70 percent to living expenses, and 20 percent for debt and contingencies. (A contingency is something unexpected, such as, "I never thought the washing machine would die this week!")

When priorities are established, budgets are drawn up, and husband and wife work together to keep the financial ship afloat, a woman experiences a deep sense of security that is critical to her well-being. There is harmony in the area of finances. True prosperity is not wealth. Prosperity is progress toward a predetermined, worthwhile goal. Too many couples decided early that their goal was wealth and the accumulation of possessions, only to discover later in life that the ladder they climbed was propped against the wrong wall all along!

True prosperity is expressed in the word *posterity*—in leaving something worthwhile built into families, children, grandchildren, great-grandchildren, and friends.

True prosperity means investing in things that will count for all mankind until Jesus, the nobleman with an inherited kingdom, comes again. If, in the budgeting of resources and time, money, and talent, we do not strive for that, we have not even begun to understand the real meaning of wealth.

Years ago, a man named Ezra Kimble taught a Sunday School class of boys. In that class was a young shoe clerk, uneducated and undistinguished, who Kimble won to Christ. This shoe clerk, D. L. Moody, became a great evangelist, and one night he preached to an audience that included the cold, indifferent pastor of a small church. In that service, F. B. Meyer caught the passion of God and Jesus Christ made evident in Moody's words and became a changed man. On one occasion Meyer spoke to a group of college students, and his message touched the heart of a man by the name of J. Wilbur Chapman who gave his life to Christ. Chapman went to work for the YMCA and called to his staff an ex-baseball player named Billy Sunday with a heart for God and a desire to proclaim His Word. Chapman set up crusades for Billy Sunday, and Sunday preached the gospel all over the world. One such crusade was scheduled in Charlotte, North Carolina, the home of an aspiring baseball player named Billy Graham. But Graham would never become famous for baseball—he would hear the words of Billy Sunday and turn his life over to Jesus Christ.

True prosperity means investing in things that will count for all mankind until Jesus comes again.

When I was called to the ministry in 1955, I looked at Billy Graham as a role model and example of what it means to be a preacher of the gospel. His love for God and his desire for men and women to come to Christ has shaped and inspired me from my earliest days as a minister. Ezra Kimble, D. L. Moody, F. B. Meyer, J. Wilbur Chapman, and Billy Sunday are all gone. They were men of another era, another generation. Yet Billy Graham stands as a part of their posterity, and through him, these men have influenced my life and the lives of countless others.

How couples spend their assets in marriage is an integral factor in the success of their relationships. But what God says about stewardship goes beyond dollars and cents. To be good stewards, a husband and wife need to learn to "do business with" the gifts God has given—financial and otherwise—in a way that will not only benefit them, but bless generations to come. May we be found faithful in all that we have.

QUESTIONS FOR FURTHER REFLECTION

1. Half of all working couples with children would choose to have the mother stay home full time if money were not an issue. Is that true of your home?

2. What is the difference between a need and a want? Do you and your mate agree on your needs and wants as a couple? How do you handle times when you disagree?

3. John Wesley encouraged his followers to make all they could, save all they could, and give all they could. Is this sound financial advice today? Why or why not?

4. Are you working to leave behind something lasting? Describe to your mate the legacy you would like to leave behind when you die, and discuss whether your financial practices support such a legacy.

13

HANDLING CONFLICT: WAR AND PEACE

I KNOW A SPOT IN NORTH CAROLINA where two rivers come together. There is a bluff high above the place where you can see them moving placidly and calmly toward their meeting point, but where they converge a battle is going on. One strong, smooth, independent stream meets an equally strong, smooth, independent stream—and the water from both churns and splashes and foams in a noisy, rushing current. From the vantage point of the bluff, it is obvious that after their somewhat violent meeting, these two bodies of water combine to form a wider, more impressive river than either was originally.

A good marriage is like this natural phenomenon. One independent person meets another independent person, and they decide to merge their lives into one. The trouble begins when they try to discover *which* one, but the truth is—it is neither. Like the rivers, two marriage partners become a new and separate creation—stronger, wider and more impressive—and one that bears the marks of both. And people do not join easily or without conflict, any more than rivers do.

MYTHS OF MARITAL CONFLICT

So many couples are surprised at the first conflicts in marriage. When they were dating there were no big problems—it was smooth sailing. Oh, there was the occasional spat or minor disagreement, but no major differences. They were so desperately in love that they never noticed they weren't "compatible." Then when they marry, it is a new ball game! It is tough to live with him. It is frustrating to deal with her. And problems arise that neither party dreamed of prior to saying, "I do."

Courtship can be amazingly conciliatory, but marriage is compulsory.

What happened? Simply this: they discovered that in dating, everything is voluntary. In marriage, everything is compulsory. Men and women alike overlook inconsistencies and irritating habits in one another prior to marriage in hopes of *attaining* marriage. They know that their cooperation and kindness is optional. If their partner becomes unreasonable, they can simply leave and give him or her plenty of time to *get* reasonable. In Shakespeare's *The Taming of the Shrew*, Petruchio courted the beautiful but difficult Katharina with a dogged determination to look past her faults:

> Say that she rail; why then I'll tell her plain
> She sings as sweetly as a nightingale:
> Say that she frown; I'll say she looks as clear
> As morning roses newly washed with dew:
> Say she be mute and will not speak a word;
> Then I'll commend her volubility,
> And say she uttereth piercing eloquence:

If she do bid me pack, I'll give her thanks,
As though she bid me stay by her a week . . .
(Act 2, Sc. 1)[1]

Walter Wangerin, Jr., wrote:

Love lies a little. Love, the desire to like and be liked,
feels so good when it is satisfied, that it never wants to
stop. Therefore, love edits the facts in order to continue
to feel good. Love allows me an innocent misconception of my fiancee, while it encourages in her a favorable misconception of myself. If it isn't blind, it does squint a bit. Love idealizes both of us.[2]

> *Good and bad marriages have very similar problems—the difference is usually in how those problems are handled.*

Courtship can be amazingly conciliatory, but in marriage the two are permanently joined, "for better or for worse, for richer or for poorer, in sickness and in health," until one of them dies. Marriage is compulsory.

So the first "marital myth" is the idea that good marriages do not have problems. All marriages have problems. In fact, good marriages and bad marriages have very similar problems—the difference is usually in how those problems are handled. Even with the increased popularity of premarital counseling and "marriage preparation" classes, many newlywed couples are still surprised when conflict comes. They should not be.

The second "marital myth" that causes harm is the belief that conflict hurts good marriages. Conflict is a part of marriage. A husband and his wife are like two porcupines that try to move closer to one another for warmth: to achieve closeness, some negotiation is required of both. How can two people believe they have a good marriage simply because they never have problems or conflicts? Often independent lifestyles can deceive people into thinking all is well (or at least tolerable.) I know more husbands and wives than I would like to admit who just coexist. They meet and communicate occasionally about their children, joint property, travel schedules, etc., and they live in a total absense of conflict—or anything else—convinced that "peace at any price" is the equivalent of a healthy union. It is not.

Both of these myths are born from the idea that conflict is always a negative thing, but in truth every conflict is simply a decision point in marriage. Conflict can become either the source of greater intimacy or the source of greater isolation. If our two porcupines would stay off by themselves, they would never have the problems that proximity could bring. And they would never know the joy of negotiating toward a deeper appreciation and understanding of one another, either.

> *Conflict can become either the source of greater intimacy or the source of greater isolation.*

A final marital myth is the notion that those who have good marriages are extremely lucky. Luck has nothing to do with good marriages or great ones. Work and self-sacrifice and patience and prayer and longsuffering and diligence and conscientiousness do—but luck does not. Texas recently voted to allow the lottery. Each week, winning combinations of numbers are published and broadcast, and the promoters of this form of gambling are quick to publicize the "lucky" winners. (One "lucky" winner was so inundated with calls from long lost friends and relatives and perpetrators of investing schemes that she disconnected her telephone, moved out of her home, and disappeared for a number of days.) Grocery store courtesy booths are crowded on paydays with people hoping to get lucky on the lottery. I am struck by the similarities between those attempting to win the lottery and those attempting to beat the divorce odds and "luck into" a happy marriage. But that is not the way it works.

Those who have been married many years would likely say that it is not actions that make or break a marriage, but reactions. Certainly actions are important, and what one proposes has the power to hurt or help the most intimate relationships. But there are marriages in trouble whose partners exhibit actions that are above reproach: they do not lie to one another, they are faithful, they do not steal—in short, they manage, for the most part, to do the right thing. But what about the unseen areas of such a union? How do the partners react in moments of great stress or conflict? How do they respond when confronted with their own short-comings? What effect does crisis have on their relationship?

If, in these crisis times, you react with jealousy, hatred, malice, coldness, or hardness, the results can be devastating. So often when someone reacts inappropriately to a situation, he excuses himself by saying, "That wasn't really me." Well then, who was it? The truth is that crisis moments or conflicts reveal the real you more accurately than any others. When pressure comes, what is inside unredeemed, uncleansed, unholy, and ungodly is prodded awake and too often released.

When you place a tea bag in a cup of cold water, nothing happens. But when you put the same tea bag into a cup of boiling water, the water turns brown. The dark color of the tea is released into the cup because of the heat of the water. The elements have not changed—tea and water—but the circumstances have. Now that the water is hot, it reveals the true nature of the tea: it is brown.

When partners are under pressure in marriage, true character is revealed, not so much in actions as in reactions. Some men and women relate to each other under stress by trading insult for insult. One woman

DEALING WITH THE INEVITABLE

> *When you are under pressure in marriage, your true character is revealed not so much in actions as in reactions.*

said to her husband: "Our marriage works because we both love the same man—you!" Another wife asked her husband, "Why do you wear your wedding ring on the wrong finger?" And he answered, "Because I married the wrong woman!" And so it goes, insult after insult. A husband looks at his wife and says, "Why did God make you so beautiful and so dumb?" And she tells him: "He made me beautiful so you could love me, and dumb so I could love you."

In Psalm 141:3 the psalmist asked God to "Set a watch, O LORD, before my mouth; keep the door of my lips." It is not essential to say all that you think. Every thought you have is not worthy of utterance. And some are certainly not beneficial to anyone. Instead of trading insult for insult, the call is to offer blessing for insult. Proverbs 15:1 says, "A gentle answer turns away wrath, but a harsh word stirs up anger." Poet and wit Ogden Nash was equally pointed in his advice:

> If you want your marriage to sizzle
> With love in the loving cup,
> Whenever you're wrong, admit it.
> Whenever you're right, shut up!

GROUND RULES FOR CONFLICT When conflict comes, and it will, remember a few ground rules. First, do not be ashamed of your anger. Everyone gets angry. So many times in marriage, opposites attract. The same differences you saw in your spouse before the two of you married that promised sparkle and zest and creativity can seem to complicate daily living after the wedding. Prize fighters frequently marry peacemakers, and when they do, conflict is tough to navigate. But anger is no sin. "Be angry," the Bible says to us, "and sin not." Anger is nothing to be ashamed of, but it needs to be handled in a mature way.

Instead of attacking the person in your anger, attack the problem. When his wife is upset and quarrelsome, a husband should ask himself a question: *Is she angry at me—or does she just need to express her frustration at a certain circumstance or problem?* If she just needs to release her emotions, respond accordingly. If you see the flash of anger in her eyes and understand that it is directed at you, consider the time and place, and if both are appropriate, sound the battle cry. There is a time for that. Good, clean, healthy arguments are the sign of a living relationship, not a dead one. Don't be ashamed of your anger.

Second, do not use what I call "heavy artillery." Remember, your conflict is an opportunity for greater intimacy or greater isolation. The choice of your weapons often determines which will result. Some couples have yet to understand that complete and unconditional victory by one party in a marital conflict is ultimately loss. Leave room for ne-

> *Complete and unconditional victory by one party in a marital conflict is ultimately loss.*

gotiation, for reconciliation. Avoid heavy artillery phrases like "I'll leave," or "Let's get a divorce, then." These are overkill. The picture of a heated argument that ends with a husband slamming the door and screaming away in the car is not an example of masculinity; it's cowardice. Use words instead that keep you in the ring, listening and learning. Do not use deadly weapons.

Third, *do not air your dirty laundry in public.* I read some time ago about a couple who held their wedding and reception in a California restaurant with 300 or so guests. As they cut their wedding cake, they began to exchange some heated words (they had just been married a few minutes!) and before the guests could figure out what the fuss was about, the restaurant became the scene of a full-fledged brawl. The groom hit the bride with a part of the wedding cake, she fired back, and then a fist fight broke out between the family and friends of the newly-wed couple. After a few minutes of total bedlam, the police arrived, but the bride and groom were nowhere to be found. This is an extreme example (most couples wait a lot longer than a few minutes for their first really colorful argument), but it makes a point. Public conflict between husbands and wives is misplaced. Disagree in private, and keep your disagreements private. Do not air your dirty laundry—not even in front of family members or close friends.

How to react when conflict comes is so critical. A woman celebrated her 50th wedding anniversary with her husband. She was a wonderful wife, mother, and grandmother, and on this special occasion, one of her grandchildren asked her the secret to her happy and enduring marriage. She smiled and said, "Well, sweetheart, when your granddaddy and I married, I made a list of ten things that I would overlook in his personality. Just ten things that I didn't like, but was willing to forgive. I decided on that day that anytime one of those ten things would come up, I would overlook it for the sake of harmony in our marriage."

One of the other grandchildren said, "Granny, tell us the list. We want to know what was on the list."

"Well, honey," she said, "to be honest with you, I never really wrote them down. But everytime your grandfather would do something that made me hopping mad, I would think to myself, 'Lucky for him that's one of the things on my list.'"

Difficulties and conflict are not the end of the world. George Washington Carver could have said, "Oh, I was born in poverty. I don't have a chance in this world to make something out of my life." Abraham Lincoln was an unsuccessful businessman and politician. His first business failed. He started a second. It failed. He had a nervous breakdown. He ran for the state legislature three times and lost all three elections. He ran for the House of Representatives twice, and lost two more races, for a political track record of 0-5. Then two runs at the senate failed, as did one vice presidential race. Someone who perseveres and survives after that kind of difficulty has what it takes to become successful. In relationships with a mate, do not "react" negatively, trading insult for insult, but react positively, trading blessing for insult. How you respond in a crisis counts.

CONFLICT THAT LEADS TO GROWTH

Author James Michener was raised on a farm. He recalls that in his growing-up years, a neighboring farmer raised apples. One day young Michener was passing by his orchards and witnessed a strange thing: the neighbor was driving nails in some of the trees in his orchard that were not bearing fruit. He watched in curiousity as this farmer approached a barren tree and drove four large, rusty nails into the base of the tree, north, south, east and west. Then he moved up higher on the trunk of the same tree and repeated the process. When he questioned the neighbor about what he was doing, he told the boy, "Just wait until next spring. You'll understand it then." And a year from that time, Michener said that apple tree, which had been unproductive, produced the biggest, richest red apples he had ever seen.

> *Some need a jolt in their marriages. They are like unproductive trees who have forgotten how to bear fruit.*

He questioned the farmer again, and got a futher explanation. "Those rusty nails," he said, "remind the tree that it was made to produce apples. Sometimes it forgets." How often, Michener wondered, was this radical treatment applied? "Only every ten years or so," the farmer replied. "Then it remembers."

Some people need a jolt in their marriages. They are like unproductive trees who have forgotten how to bear fruit. What "rusty nails" could wake up relationships before they become hopelessly barren? What are the signs of a marriage that no longer produces fruit in season?

I believe that the book of Ephesians shows four "heart stages" in marriage recognized chiefly in the "rusty nail" of conflict.

> Therefore, laying aside falsehood, speak truth, each one of you, with his neighbor, for we are members of one another. Be angry, and yet do not sin; do not let the sun go down on your anger, and do not give the devil opportunity. Let him who steals steal no longer; but rather let him labor, performing with his own hands what is good, in order that he may have something to share with him who has need. Let no unwholesome word proceed from your mouth, but only such a word as is good for edification according to the need of the moment, that it may give grace to those who hear. (Eph. 4:25-29)

Stage One: The Bruised Heart

Sometimes arguments begin because people neglect their mates. Sometimes they begin—let's be honest here—because they plan to argue with their mates. (I actually planned my first "married fight" with JoBeth. I was preaching on handling marital conflict as a brand new husband and pastor and foolishly decided I was short on experience!) Sometimes arguments begin because something has taken place that one person does not like. And hearts get bruised.

But no matter how an argument begins, it is possible to be angry and not sin. The critical question is one of time and duration. How can a bruised heart be kept from becoming a serious affliction? The answer, according to Paul, is not to let the sun go down on the anger.

Bruised hearts are a fact of life. But people are not to keep hammering away at one another when their hearts are in this state. Before they go to sleep at night, and although they may not agree, a point of reconciliation must be reached. (Notice I said reconciliation—not necessarily resolution. Whether there is agreement on the issue at hand or not, a couple needs to agree that each is for the other, before all else.) A bruised heart is the first stage of marital conflict, but the anger that accompanies it can be kept from becoming sin if its duration is limited.

The second stage of marital conflict is what I call the cold heart stage. It naturally follows when the bruised heart is allowed to fester. Perhaps some are very familiar with this stage. An argument begins and hearts are bruised. Both parties go to sleep with no attempt at reconciliation. The next day is a chilly one. One is polite. The other is cautious. The one is conciliatory, but with a note of cynicism in his voice. One or both partners think of past offenses, replaying them silently like old home videos, perhaps recalling the most recent ones out loud. Where do a husband and wife find relief for the cold heart? By speaking words that give—this is the operative word—grace to those who hear. What is grace? Undeserved favor. By grace full words, actions, and attitudes, the cold heart can be melted.

Stage Two: The Cold Heart

If grace is not applied to a cold heart, it becomes a hard heart. What does a hard heart look like? Paul describes it as grieving the Holy Spirit. This is getting serious, is it not? A simple argument resulted in a bruised heart. No reconciliation came, and the heart grew cold. Grace was not applied, and the cold heart became a hard heart that is bitter, angry, and revengeful.

Stage Three: The Hard Heart

And this grieves not just the parties directly involved, but the third person of the Trinity—the Holy Spirit Himself. He has to work on husband and wife at this stage, saying to husbands, "You are to initiate love; you are to initiate forgiveness." But the husband's hard heart may say, "I'm not giving in this time. I'm right. I've put up with this as long as I can, and I'm putting my foot down." To the wife He says, "You are to respond in love

and forgiveness to your husband, as you would to Me."
But the wife says, "No way. I'm going to give him the
silent treatment. I'll show him I don't need him or
anyone else."

Things have heated up, have they not? Too much
time has passed. Too little grace has been given. Now
the Holy Spirit is grieved and has to tenderize two hard
hearts. After 30-plus years of marriage, I am knowl-
edgeable about the bruised heart stage, and I know
something of the cold heart stage. I have not spent
much time in the hard heart stage, but I am not a total
stranger to it.

When you and your spouse are in this stage of
conflict, let me suggest a principle that may help. I call
it CLASP. It is an acrostic for some simple, recom-
mended behaviors that should cool things down if they
are applied correctly.

C: Calm down. It is amazing how heated and intense things can become in just a short time. Take a
deep breath. Try to relax. If you are anxious or agitated,
you will not make much headway at finding some
common ground.

L: Lower your voice. Shouting does not prove a
point with any more certainty than a quiet word can.
Take it down a couple of octaves. You will be surprised
at how just these two simple steps can defuse a heated
moment.

A: Ask some questions. Now that you have calmed
down and stopped shouting, real communication is
possible. Ask your mate to reestablish his or her position. Do not debate anything, or try to justify your own
position. Just ask, listen, and seek to understand.

S: State your position. You have asked for clarification from your mate. Now give him or her your perspective again in a calm, quiet manner. Strive for
understanding. Avoid accusatory words. You are not in
court. You are at home.

P: Propose a solution. Work together to find one that is mutually acceptable, reasonable and workable. Do not give up until you have proposed something both can agree to at least try.

CLASP is a tool to employ to avoid the fourth stage of marital conflict, the indifferent heart. It has been said that the opposite of love is not hate but indifference. I would have to agree. In the indifferent heart stage, the partners are beyond conflict. They just do not care anymore. They are too weary or numb to try to resolve their differences. At one time hearts were only bruised, but neither party dealt with it. Hearts grew cold, and grace was not given a chance to work. Cold hearts became hard hearts, and even the leading of the Holy Spirit of God was rejected.

Stage Four: The Indifferent Heart

Is there a way out of the indifferent heart stage? Yes! It requires the exercise of the will by might: "And be kind to one another, tenderhearted, forgiving each other, just as God in Christ also has forgiven you" (Eph. 4:32). Time has passed on. Grace was ignored. The Holy Spirit was rejected. Now an act of will is required. Two indifferent hearts must choose to be tender and forgiving.

The fourth stage of the heart in marital conflict is a tough, tough place to be. No one is trained to handle this kind of crisis in a marriage. If you were learning to fly a plane, a first area of instruction would be what to do in case of an emergency. You might chafe at this a bit, but even despite a desire to "get on with it" and fly, you would listen. Because to fail at flying is a life or death thing. Why are people less afraid of marital failure? It somehow does not seem as permanent, but its scars are lasting ones.

IS THE SIZZLE GONE? Perhaps for some reading this book, the apathetic stage is home base. There is no more emotion. Marriage is not a relationship; it is an exercise in endurance. Others might say they are not indifferent, but at times the spark is missing. Love, like the economy, does not stay at a constant level. There are depressions, recessions, and inflationary periods. Certainly there are mountaintops and valleys in love. And when you are in the valley, you know that something vital is missing. How do you get it back? I think you begin with some very practical measures.

Marital love is a committed act of the will before it is anything else. It is sacrifical love, . . a no-turning-back decision.

First, confess that you did not really understand marital love. Confess ignorance! Say to God and to one another that your knowledge of marriage was incomplete. You understood violins and flowers and romance—and those are a part of the whole—but you did not grasp the weight of the word *commitment*. Marital love is a committed act of the will before it is anything else. It is sacrifical love—love without any expectation of "return-on-investment." It is a no-turning-back decision. Some would say, quite honestly, that they did not understand this up front. So the first thing to do to bring the feeling and emotion back is to confess our limited understanding of sacrificial married love.

Second, believe that God Himself can bring love back into any marriage. R. C. Sproul has said, "The issue of faith is not so much whether we believe in God, but whether we believe the God we believe in." You have to believe that God can do it. Belief is hardest when it applies personally. People can believe that God created the world or that He parted the Red Sea for the people of Israel. They can believe the virgin birth and the resurrection and subconsciously trust Him for their next breath and heartbeat, but what about breathing life into a lifeless marriage? The prophet Jeremiah asked the question, "Is there anything that God cannot do?" The answer is no—not one thing! You have to believe that the God who has done and is doing impossible things can bring love back into the marital relationship.

To believe that the God you believe in can bring back the joy and spontaneity marriage once held is not enough. You must begin in faith to demonstrate acts of love, even when the feeling of love is not there. You cannot wait until the feeling is there to demonstrate it—that would not be faith! Put into action what you hope to feel. Is this hypocritical? No! It is evidence of unconditional commitment—the very definition of love. Imagine how you would act if the loving feelings you once had for your mate returned, then act that way.

There is one final thing if your marriage has gone flat, and that is, to forgive and ask forgiveness—regularly, sincerely, and as completely as you know how. You will be surprised at what may take place.

IF YOU ARE READY TO GIVE UP

Maybe your marriage has done more than lose its spark. You are all too familiar with the stages of the heart in marital conflict—especially stage four. You may be contemplating separation or divorce. If this is where you are today—please do one more thing. (And if this isn't you, by the way, you know people for whom this suggestion will be relevant.) First, get an alarm clock that ticks. An old-fashioned one. (A digital clock is not as good for our purpose. You need to hear the seconds going by.) Set two chairs very close to one another in a room where you will not be disturbed. Then make a commitment with your mate to set aside 30 minutes a day for six days to meet together in the place you have made. Surely even the most battered marriage is worth a 30-minute effort.

On the first day, and each subsequent day, sit down facing your spouse and set the alarm on the clock to go off in thirty minutes. For the first five minutes, be absolutely silent. During this time, think about what it would be like to live alone. Imagine living without your partner for the rest of your life. Imagine the loss of friendships that have been forged during your marriage. Friends of couples who separate are always forced to take sides at some point. Some will bail out altogether. The aftermath of a divorce can be incredibly lonely. Contemplate your future totally alone.

For the second five minutes, think only about the role you have played in your marital difficulties. Stop judging the other person; assess your responsibility in the situation only. Take ownership of your shortcomings, your faults, the hurtful things that you have said and done.

For the third five minutes, focus on your children. Anyone who imagines that children are not permanently scarred in divorce is sadly mistaken. Imagine the loss that your choice to separate would inflict on your children. Imagine being a single parent and living with the limitations that entails. Think about your children.

For the fourth five minutes, open your Bibles to I Corinthians 13 and read the most accurate description of love ever written. Read it out loud. "Love is patient, love is kind and is not jealous; love does not brag and is not arrogant . . ." Let one partner read aloud one day, the other the next. Think about what you hear.

During the fifth five minutes, play the nostalgia game. Verbally recall times that you felt close to one another. Maybe you will remember a time that you walked on the beach early one morning holding hands. Or a time that a child was sick and you took turns holding that child throughout the night. For five minutes, remember out loud the moments that cemented your love for one another.

Finally, take five minutes to pray. Tell God what you think is wrong with your marriage and confess your part in it. Let one partner pray, then the other. Ask His forgiveness for the times you know you missed the mark when it comes to loving your spouse.

Why a ticking clock? Because with every tick you will be reminded of the brevity of life and sense the urgency to resolve what is wrong between you. And because in each tick you will begin to hear the clock saying, "Self-self-self-self-self-self-self . . .," and understand that there is only one person in your marriage you can change: you. Reject the tendency to allow conflict to become a source of isolation. Instead, commit to make it a source of greater intimacy between you and your mate.

QUESTIONS FOR FURTHER REFLECTION

1. Do you believe that a healthy marriage is always free of conflict? What about your spouse?
2. Discuss together the following statement: "Conflict can become either the source of greater intimacy or the source of greater isolation." Which has been more true of conflict in your marriage thus far?
3. Review the "ground rules for conflict" on pages 194-95. Would it be worthwhile to adopt them in your marriage? Are you willing to do so?
4. How would using the "CLASP" principle on page 200 help during times of conflict? Which aspect of it would be most difficult for you? For your spouse?

14

THE ESSENTIAL
INGREDIENT:
JESUS CHRIST

WHEN PEOPLE ASK WHAT I DO, I LIKE to say that I am in the relationship business. I am. And so is the church. We are in the business of helping people establish right relationships with God and right relationships with others. A book on marriage and the home would be sadly incomplete without this final chapter. Because no matter how brilliant the partners, no matter how strong their love, no matter how committed they are to their union, the odds against a marriage even surviving "in name only" is little more than a 50-50 proposition without some serious help.

> *Horizontal relationships—relationships between people—are crippled at the outset unless the vertical relationship—the relationship between each person and God—is in place.*

Horizontal relationships—relationships between people—are crippled at the outset unless the vertical relationship—the relationship between each person and God—is in place. Trying to make a marriage sizzle without God is like trying to put together a 3,000-piece jigsaw puzzle with the wrong picture on the box top. The odds of success are very, very slim.

Every bride and groom who stand at the altar have, for just a few moments after they are pronounced husband and wife, a perfect union. For a few moments marriage is unmarred by conflict or selfishness or dishonesty. But that perfection never lasts, because every marriage is an enterprise undertaken by two imperfect people. Expectations are dashed. Lifelong dreams die. The ideal husband or wife and the husband or wife you marry are two different people, as this rather humorous look at love and marriage by Bob Phillips proves:

The Ideal Husband: What Every Woman Expects:

- He will be a brilliant conversationalist.

- A very sensitive man—kind and understanding, truly loving.

- A very hard-working man.

- A man who helps around the house by washing dishes, vacuuming floors, and taking care of the yard.

- Someone who helps his wife raise the children.

- A man of emotional and physical strength.

- A man who is as smart as Einstein, but looks like Robert Redford.

What She Gets:

- He always takes her to the best restaurants. Some day he may even take her inside.

- He doesn't have any ulcers; he gives them.

- Anytime he has an idea in his head, he has the whole thing in a nutshell.

- He's a well-known miracle worker—it's a miracle when he works.

- He supports his wife in the manner to which she was accustomed—he's letting her keep her job.

- He's such a bore that he even bores you to death when he gives you a compliment.

- He has occasional flashes of silence that make his conversation brilliant.

The Ideal Wife: What Every Man Expects

- Always beautiful and cheerful. Could have married a movie star, but wanted only you. Hair that never needs curlers or beauty shops.

- Beauty that won't run in a rainstorm. Never sick— just allergic to jewelry and fur coats.

- Insists that moving furniture by herself is good for her figure.

- Expert in cooking, cleaning house, fixing the car or tv, painting the house and keeping quiet.

- Favorite hobbies: mowing the lawn and shoveling snow.

- Hates charge cards.

- Her favorite expression: "What can I do for you, dear?"

- Thinks you have Einstein's brain but look like Mr. Universe.

- Wishes you would go out with the boys so she could get some sewing done.

- Loves you because you are so sexy.

What He Gets:

- She speaks 140 words a minute with gusts up to 180.

- She was once a model for a totem pole.

- A light eater: as soon as it gets light, she starts eating.

- Where's there's smoke, there she is—cooking.

- She lets you know you only have two faults: everything you say and everything you do.

- No matter what she does with it, her hair looks like an explosion in a steel wool factory.

- If you get lost, open your wallet. She'll find you.[1]

Always in marriage there is a difference between the expectation and the reality. C. S. Lewis said that one of the miracles of love, however, is that "it gives . . . a power of seeing through its own enchantments and yet not being disenchanted."

Once, too, in the garden of Eden, the vertical relationship between God and man was as clean and unbroken as a minute-old marriage. But then sin entered the picture, and with it shame and dishonesty and fear and anger. Man was no longer naked and innocent—he was clothed and covered—not just in leaves, but in guilt. Instead of living each day in unmarred fellowship with their Maker, the first man and woman hid from Him, questioning His love for them and knowing that their's for Him was far from perfect.

What does this ancient story have to do with modern marriage? The answer is everything. It means that all are sinners, and because of that fact, separated from God. The vertical relationship with Him is broken, and in and of yourself, you can do nothing to remedy that fact. You cannot restore your relationship with God. You cannot change the past. The things that you have done that were rebellious and disobedient in the sight of God are done—and they cannot be undone. No matter how bad or how vile, you cannot remake the past to improve your standing before a holy God.

> *You cannot restore your relationship with God, and I cannot restore mine. We cannot change the past.*

Neither can you control the future. You cannot say, "Okay, God, from this day forward, I promise to do everything right. Starting today, God, you can always count on me." You would be foolish to try. The past cannot be changed —it's done, and we cannot change the future either—considering the past track record of holiness. All are in a reconcilable position where God is concerned.

That is the bad news. But the good news is this: God has done what you could not. He—the offended party—has sent his Son, Jesus Christ, to be the peace offering He requires. His Son lived and suffered and died on a cross, and His shed blood became our atonement when He said, "It is finished!" Through Him, all can be reconciled to God once and for all time.

> *God has done what you and I could not: sent His Son to be the peace offering He requires.*

When we confess our sin, turn from our sin, and invite Jesus Christ to come into our life, our vertical relationship with Him is permanently and perfectly established. He covers the past that we could not change with His blood, and the future that we could not control is in His hands. Jesus verified this fact when he said, "I give eternal life to them, and they shall never perish; and no one shall snatch them out of my hand. My Father, who has given them to Me, is greater than all; and no one is able to snatch them out of the Father's hand"(John 10:28-29). Eternity with Him is sealed.

But trusting Christ does not impact only on the past and the future. It makes a difference in the very present, giving each one an unshakeable identity. As Paul wrote in his letter to the Roman Christians:

> For all who are being led by the Spirit of God, these are sons of God. For you have not received a spirit of slavery leading to fear again, but you have received a spirit of adoption as sons by which we cry out, "Abba! Father!" The Spirit Himself bears witness with our spirit that we are children of God, and if children, heirs also, heirs of God and fellow heirs with Christ, if indeed we suffer with Him in order that we may also be glorified with Him. (Rom. 8:14-17)

Most serious marriage problems that I have seen were rooted at some point in difficulty with self-esteem. If you would rather be anyone other than yourself, you have a self-esteem problem. Most people carry pictures of their family in wallets or pocketbooks. We show them to friends (or even near strangers) on request or when the conversation turns to family. "These are my boys," someone might say. "This is my wife." It really gets serious when you get a group of folks together and the talk turns to *grand*children. Look out! And you get excited to hear someone say, "That's a fine looking family you have there. I know you must be proud of them."

But have you ever been in a group where people started showing one another the pictures on their driver's licenses? In fact, I am not sure how anyone recognizes us with that poor image as a reference. Most are extremely critical of themselves and do not like to call attention to their pictures, much less their person.

How did we get in this mess of poor self-esteem? From the moment a doctor slaps a baby's bottom and places him in his mother's arms, self-esteem is formed. Psychologists tell us that a child's basic image of himself and how he relates to others is formed by the time he is five or six. Imagine the damage to this young person if he is confronted early in life with abandonment, abuse, or ridicule.

But even in these cases, all is not lost. Your self-image need not be permanently damaged by the circumstances of life. It can be recast when there is an infusion of new life in Jesus Christ. You can literally be changed. "Therefore if any man is in Christ," Paul wrote, "he is a new creature; the old things passed away; behold, new things have come." A lovely, adequate self-image can be built anew, regardless of the former environment.

Jesus Christ can make eternity certain and restore identity—and both are important to marriage. But perhaps most significant to the marital relationship is that when you come to know Him you receive His Holy Spirit, and with it the power to shatter enmity between yourself and those you live with and love. I do not know of a single relationship that would not be helped tremendously by the fruit of the Holy Spirit, the evidence of His presence in a life: "But the fruit of the Spirit is love, joy, peace, patience, kindness, goodness, gentleness, self-control; against such things there is no law" (Gal. 5:22).

Your self image need not be permanently damaged by the circumstances of life. It can be recast when there is an infusion of new life in Jesus Christ.

The third person of the Trinity is a reconciler. Before you knew Jesus Christ and were reconciled with God, you had a spirit of rebellion. All were rebellious before God and in hopeless conflict with others. But with faith comes release from that bondage:

For the law of the Spirit of life in Christ Jesus has set you free from the the law of sin and death. For what the law could not do, weak as it was through the flesh, God did: sending His own Son in the likeness of sinful flesh and as an offering for sin. He condemned sin in the flesh in order that the requirement of the Law might be fulfilled in us, who do not walk according to the flesh but according to the Spirit. For those who are according to the flesh have set their minds on the things of the flesh, but those who are according to the Spirit, the things of the Spirit. For the mind set on the flesh is death, but the mind set on the Spirit is life and peace (Rom. 8: 2-6).

Once you were rebellious against God, and therefore in competition with one another in the marital arena. How could you hope to have peace and harmony and intimacy in homes and marriages if you had no peace? But when you are reconciled to God through Jesus Christ and He gives you His Holy Spirit, you can be reconciled to one another. Without Him, you have no hope of maintaining right relationships with one another.

LIFE'S THREE BIG QUESTIONS Most, consciously or unconsciously, have been asking three basic questions of themselves for a long time. All answer them with lifestyles and attitudes, but the questions are very simply these:

- How do I look?
- How am I doing?
- How important am I?

The first question has to with perception. How am I perceived by others? The second has to do with performance. Am I performing well? Am I measuring up to the right standards? The final question has to do with status. Am I important? How important, compared to others that I know? These three things—perception, performance, and status—affect most of the decisions you make in your life, including who you marry and what you expect from marriage. Until you allow God to answer these questions and believe what He tells you, you will very likely make a mess of things trying to get your own answers.

To illustrate this, look at a modern man who has, in all likelihood, spent a great deal of time asking himself these questions. His name is

> *Three things-perception, performance and status-affect most of the decisions you make in your lives including who you marry and what you expect from marriage.*

Donald Trump. Unless you have been sleeping for the last five years or so, his name will be quite familiar. How do you think Donald Trump judges his appearance? How does Donald look to Donald? I believe the response would be positive. "I look good," he might say. "All my suits are custom made, and I have a great tan from skiing year round. Ivana is behind me now, and I have a new beauty who finds me attractive. Her name is Marla—Marla Maples? Maybe you have seen her on Broadway."

How does Donald think he is doing? "Well," he might answer, "just look at all my toys. I have a lot of stuff for my efforts—and most of it has my name on it. There's Trump Tower, Trump Plaza, Trump Mansion, the Trump Taj Mahal, Trump Airlines—I mean, could I do much better?"

How important does Donald Trump think he is? "For that," I can imagine him saying, "you'll have to check my Dun and Bradstreet rating."

But now, if reports are accurate, perhaps Mr. Trump is reassessing his answers to these questions—or at least his way of arriving at those answers. The "he-who-dies-with-the-most-toys-wins" philosophy is only comforting when you have more toys than anyone else in the game. When you do not, self-worth is bound to take a beating, because the standard used to measure it fluctuates constantly. Allowing the world to shape self-esteem is a dangerous thing.

Where can you get accurate answers to those questions? How do I look? How am I doing? How important am I? The world cannot tell you with any degree of certainty. Your mate cannot even completely reflect the truth. I believe the best answers come from God and are recorded in His Word. If you opened the Bible and asked God for the truth about how you look, He might direct you to the words of David in Psalm 139:

> For Thou didst form my inward parts; Thou didst weave me in my mother's womb. I will give thanks to Thee, for I am fearfully and wonderfully made; wonderful are Thy works, and my soul knows it well. My frame was not hidden from Thee when I was made in secret, and skillfully wrought in the depths of the earth. Thine eyes have seen my unformed substance; and in Thy book they were all written, the days that were ordained for me, when as yet there was not one of them. (Ps. 139:13-16)

God sees each one as fearfully and wonderfully and beautifully made by divine prescription—put together by none other than God Almighty. He has plans for you—and a unique message that He wants to deliver to the world through your very life.

What if you asked God how you are doing? By what standard would He measure performance? The prophet Micah says there is no guesswork involved here:

> He has told you, O man, what is good; and what does the LORD require of you but to do justice, to love kindness, and to walk humbly with your God?
> (Micah 6:8)

Do justice. Love mercy. Walk humbly before God. You mean no Trump Towers required? Not for God. The performance He seeks is of a quieter caliber.

Does God have any answer to the final question, the question of status or significance? You bet He does. How important are you to Him? Unbelievably important. Just look:

> For God so loved the world that He gave His only begotten Son, that whosoever believes in Him should not perish, but have eternal life. (John 3:16)

That is how important you are. He loved you before you were born, and never wanted to spend eternity (or a moment of His life) without you. When your sin made a relationship with Him impossible, He bought you back by the blood of His own sinless Son. "God demonstrated His own love for us," wrote the apostle Paul, "in that while we were yet sinners, Christ died for us" (Rom. 5:8).

How important are you? So important that God gave all that He had to give for you—and would have given it still, were you the only person on this earth.

How important are you? So important that God gave all that He had to give for you—and would have given it still, were you the only person on this earth. It is almost impossible to fathom. It is too big and too powerful to grasp, and yet so simple a child can understand the central truth of it. Peter Kreeft writes, "Why did God create you? He created billions of other people; were they not enough for Him? No, they were not. He had to have you. He will not rest until He has you home."

FREEDOM IN CHRIST

Our society loves the word "choice." Modern men and women insist on the right to choose abortion, to choose infidelity, to choose multiple marriages, to choose bits and pieces of convenient religions for a do-it-yourself deal. But each of those choices leads not to freedom, but to bondage. Only one choice leads to freedom, and that is to choose Jesus Christ. In that choice is total freedom unlike any other that the world has to offer.

> If you abide in my word, then you are truly disciples of Mine; and you shall know the truth, and the truth shall make you free. Truly, truly, I say to you, everyone who commits sin is the slave of sin. And the slave does not remain in the house forever; the son does remain forever. If therefore the Son shall make you free, you shall be free indeed. (John 8:31-32; 34-36)

In Him there is freedom from the past, freedom from fear, and freedom from habit. The past can no longer haunt you when you are in Christ. His blood covers all that it contains, and it holds no power over you anymore. You are free from the fear of not measuring up, because He has said that He is able to present you spotless before God. And you are free from the harness of old habits that keep you from moving on in life and being what He made you to be. G. K. Chesterton understood this when he wrote, "The more I considered Christianity, the more I found that while it had established a rule and order, the chief aim of that order was to give room for good things to run wild."

God never intended a marriage to be commonplace, hum drum, or boring.

Marriage is one good thing created by God that He establishes parameters around in order to allow it to "run wild." He never intended marriage to be commonplace, humdrum, tired, or boring.

> Thus in love the free-lovers say: "Let us have the splendour of offering ourselves without the peril of committing ourselves; let us see whether we can commit suicide an unlimited number of times." Emphatically, it will not work. There are thrilling moments, doubtless, for the spectator, the amateur, the aesthete; but there is one thrill that is known only to the soldier

who fights for his own flag, to the ascetic who starves himself for his own illumination, to the lover who finally makes his own choice. And it is this transfiguring self-discipline that makes a vow a truly sane thing. . . . All around us the city of small sins, abounding in backways and retreats, but surely, sooner or later, the towering flame will rise from the harbour announcing that the reign of cowards is over and a man is burning his ships."[2]

If you and your mate have not done so, burn your ships today. Plan a future lived out together totally committed to one another by the grace of God in Christ Jesus. Few things in the world hold more exiting possibilities than the union of one man with one woman for life. With its twists and turns, life is a roller coaster ride not meant for the fearful or faint of heart. Lived out with Jesus Christ, it is a great adventure. And embarked upon with a mate whose heart belongs to Him as well, it is the adventure of a lifetime.

QUESTIONS FOR FURTHER REFLECTION

1. How have your expectations of what marriage would be and the reality of it been different? What one thing about marriage surprised you most?

2. What difference does a personal relationship with Jesus Christ make in the life of a husband or a wife?

3. How does healthy self-esteem give life to a marriage?

4. Consider G. K. Chesterton's statement that the chief aim of Christianity's order is to "give room for good things to run wild." Discuss how God's rules for marriage and the family free us to enjoy them to the fullest.

How to Use
Romancing the Home
for Study

Applying the principles and suggestions presented in *Romancing the Home* can enrich any marriage. Each chapter contains questions designed for creative interpretations and responses. These questions encourage you to explore options and make personal applications.

Whether you choose to study *Romancing the Home* as an individual, with your spouse, or in a group, you will discover how to apply God's principles for marriage through your study. To purchase additional copies of *Romancing the Home* check with your local Christian bookstore.

A one-on-one time of study and dialogue will help you and your spouse discover how to have a marriage that sizzles.

Suggestions for Couples

Two-week Begin with chapter 1 and for the next two weeks study
Intensive Study a chapter each day. Commit to a two-week period and
avoid making plans outside the home that might interrupt your study. Make a date with your spouse—choose
a specific time to meet each day. Early morning or late
evening sessions are good choices for the fourteen-day,
fourteen-chapter study.

- Read a chapter before you meet.
- Begin your time together with prayer.
- Review the chapter. Highlight important points you
  learned in private study.
- Discuss the questions related to each chapter. See
  what your spouse has learned and how you can be
  sensitive to what he or she needs in the relationship.
- Discuss any difficulties discovered in your marriage.
  Set specific goals for overcoming the difficulties.
- Celebrate the places where your marriage already
  sizzles. Make plans to do something special to rein-
  force those feelings.
- End your study with prayer each day.

Fourteen-week If your schedule doesn't allow for an intensive study,
Study you may want to consider this alternative. Select one
day a week for the study and begin a fourteen-week
study together. Use a calendar to schedule the time.

- Before your weekly meeting read a chapter and
  answer the questions related to that chapter. Exchange answers with your spouse. See what your
  spouse has learned and how you can be sensitive to
  what he or she needs in the relationship. Choose one
  or two specific needs and focus on those during the
  coming week.
- Begin your time together with prayer. You may want
  to keep a prayer diary to record specific prayer
  requests and answers to prayer that have grown out
  of your study together.

- Review the chapter. Highlight important points you learned in private study.
- Discuss any difficulties discovered in your marriage. Set specific goals for overcoming the difficulties.
- Celebrate the places where your marriage already sizzles. Make plans to do something special to reinforce those feelings.
- End your study with prayer each day.

Romancing the Home can be an excellent study tool for groups. Here are a few settings and suggested approaches.

SUGGESTIONS FOR GROUPS

A weekend retreat (Friday evening through Saturday noon) provides couples with time away and an opportunity to learn more about marriage. Enlist several people to find an appropriate site for the study. An accommodating home, campsite, hotel, or resort are a few possibilities. Select a guest speaker or couple to facilitate the study. Remember to keep your agenda flexible and build in time for romance!

Couples' Retreat

- Begin the retreat on Friday night with a casual dinner.
- Session 1 (7-9:00 p.m. with a break), Part One: Ho-Hum Husbands and Worn-Out Wives.
- Begin the day on Saturday with a casual, buffet breakfast and a time of prayer together.
- Session 2 (8-9:30 a.m. with a break), Part Two: Preparing the Kindling.
- Session 3 (10 a.m.-noon), Part Three: Fanning the Flames.

This meeting can take place at a church or in a home for a period of three or four months and will provide fellowship in addition to a study about marriage. This group can include a mix of couples preparing for marriage, couples married for less than two years, cou-

Week-night Study Group

ples married for two to twenty years, or couples celebrating forty or more years of marriage. On the other hand, you might want to concentrate on specific groups. *Romancing the Home* has proven itself particularly useful as a marriage preparation study.

- Select or enlist a group leader/facilitator.
- Plan for light refreshments prior to or following the meeting.
- Assign one chapter and study questions per week in advance to individual couples for presentation to the group.
- A prepared leader can provide additional information when needed.
- Each couple should read and study the chapter and answer the questions prior to the meeting.
- Begin each session with a time of prayer.
- Review the chapter and study questions.
- Discuss problem areas in marriage and specific ways to solve problems.
- Discuss practical ways to improve relationships and rekindle the fire in marriage.
- Stick to the subject at hand. Some couples will want to turn the agenda into a personal counseling session and this will detract from the purpose of the study.
- Remember to keep the focus on solutions, not problems.
- Conclude with prayer and assignments for the following meeting.

Sunday or Wednesday Night Study at the Church

A one-hour study each week can be scheduled for one quarter or extended for a longer period of time. The leader should be sensitive to the needs of the group and attentive when they make suggestions. Making affirmations when possible will encourage participation. Books for each couple should be available. The church office should be notified in advance of any study material needs. Follow the plan suggested for the fourteen-week study.

Some women enjoy spending time with their neighbors. Combining fellowship with practical study can meet a felt need. Locate child-care facilities for one morning a week. Begin a four-month study at 10:00 a.m. and conclude with a carry-in lunch. Other options include picking the children up at noon and going to a local park for a sack lunch if the weather permits. The leader/teacher can be enlisted from the neighborhood or subdivision, but careful attention should be given to the qualifications.

Neighborhood Morning Study for Homemakers

- Read each chapter before you meet.
- Plan for light refreshments before your meeting.
- Begin your time together with prayer.
- Review the chapter. Allow each person to highlight important principles she learned from her study.
- Discuss the questions related to each chapter.
- Discuss the difficulties in marriage. Brainstorm specific ways to overcome those difficulties.
- Encourage participants to celebrate places where their marriage already sizzles.
- Find ways to encourage one another to strengthen their marriages.
- End your study with prayer each day. Commit to pray for a specific individual in the group for the next week.

The book can be adapted to a nine-month study, meeting for two hours once a month. Women's groups which meet during the school year could use this approach. Enlist a guest speaker from the community to address each topic. Encourage members to invite their neighbors to attend. A suggested study plan is:

Nine-month Study

- September: overview of marriage and family (chaps. 1 and 2).

- October: goal setting, roles of husband and wife (chaps. 3 through 5).
- November: affection and sex (chaps. 6 and 7).
- December: communication and recreation (chaps. 8 and 9).
- January: how to be an attractive wife (chap. 10).
- February: making your home a haven (chap. 11).
- March: finances (chap. 12).
- April: handling conflict (chap.13).
- May: a Christ-centered marriage (chap. 14).

SUGGESTIONS FOR INDIVIDUAL STUDY

Occasionally an individual wants to take the initiative to put sizzle back into the marriage. A morning quiet time, lunchtime at work, weekends alone, and other opportunities can provide time for study. If you want more from marriage, you can study this book with personal application in mind.

- Be willing to ask yourself probing questions like, "What is it like being married to me?" "What can I do to help my companion enjoy our marriage again?" Other personal questions can be applied to the study.
- If your spouse does not seem enthusiastic about your marriage, pray for that person and ask God to provide His direction in bringing romance back into the home.

A FINAL WORD

Whether you use *Romancing the Home* for individual study, with your spouse, or in a group setting, I pray that the Lord will use that time to renew and strengthen your relationship with Him and with your spouse.

NOTES

Introduction

1. Cecil Osborne, *The Art of Understanding Your Mate* (Grand Rapids, Mich.: Zondervan Publishing House, 1970), 39.

2. G. K. Chesterton, *Irish Impressions* (New York: John Lane Company, 1920).

Chapter 1

1. "Once upon a Time, from the First Kiss to the Final Break—the Twelve Years of Charles and Diana," *Life* magazine, February 1993, 36, 39.

2. "A Defense of Rash Vows," *Brave New Family, G. K. Chesterton on Men and Women, Children, Sex, Divorce, Marriage and the Family* (Ignatius Press, 1990), 49.

3. Mike Mason, *The Mystery of Marriage* (Portland, Oreg.: Multnomah Press, 1985), 54.

4. "Heretics" in *Collected Works of G. K. Chesterton*, vol. 1 (San Francisco, Calif.: Ignatius Press, 1986), 136-45.

Chapter 2

1. Mike Mason, *The Mystery of Marriage* (Portland, Oreg.: Multnomah Press, 1985), 34-35.

2. Ibid., 144.

3. Zig Ziglar, *Courtship After Marriage* (Nashville, Tenn.: Oliver Nelson Books, 1990), 224.

4. Paraphrased from "The Seven Ages of the Cold," *The Saturday Evening Post*, December 31, 1955.

Chapter 3

1. Mike Mason, *The Mystery of Marriage* (Portland, Oreg.: Multnomah Press, 1985), 60-61.

2. George Gendron, "Schwarzkopf on Leadership," editorial, *Inc.* magazine, January 1992, vol. 14, no. 1, 11.

3. Garry Friesen, *Decision Making and the Will of God, a Biblical Alternative to the Traditional View* (Portland, Oreg.: Multnomah Press, 1980), 304.

4. Robert Browning, "Rabbi Ben Ezra,"*Browning Poetical Works 1833-1864,* Ian Jack, editor (London: Oxford University Press, 1970).

5. Leonard Ravenhill, source unknown.

6. "The Magic of Herman Miller," *Industry Week,* Feb. 18, 1991, 12-17.

Chapter 4

1. "The Thing," *Collected Works of G. K. Chesterton* (San Francisco: Ignatius Press, 1990).

Chapter 5

1. Samuel J. Stone and Samuel S. Wesley, "The Church's One Foundation," public domain.

2. Mike Mason, *The Mystery of Marriage* (Portland, Oreg.: Multnomah Press, 1985), 138.

3. Maisie Ward, *Gilbert Keith Chesterton* (New York: Sheed & Ward, 1943), 104-5.

4. Deitrich Bonhoeffer, "A Wedding Sermon from a Prison Cell, May 1943," *Letters and Papers from Prison* (New York: Collier Books Macmillan Publishing Company, 1953), 43-44.

Chapter 6

1. Willard Harley, *His Needs, Her Needs* (Grand Rapids, Mich.: Fleming H. Revell, a division of Baker Book House Company), 10.

2. C. S. Lewis, *The Four Loves* (Orlando, Fla.: Harcourt Brace Jovanovich, Publishers), 57.

3. "The Hug," source unknown.

4. Lewis, 57.

5. Robert McGee, *The Search for Significance* (Houston, Tex.: Rapha Publishing, 1990), 407.

Chapter 7

1. Abigail Van Buren, "Tired in Lincoln, Nebraska," *Dear Abby,* the *Chicago Tribune,* July 14, 1992.

2. Jim Sanderson, syndicated columnist, 1981, Sun Features, Inc., used by permission.

3. Mike Mason, *The Mystery of Marriage* (Portland, Oreg.: Multnomah Press, 1985), 125.

Chapter 8

1. Frederick Buechner, *A Room Called Remember* (New York: Harper & Row, Publishers, Inc., 1984), 172.

Chapter 9

1. David Broder, "Messages Bear Out Quayle's Warning: the American Family Is Threatened," *Houston Chronicle,* March 29, 1993.

2. "Dan Quayle Was Right," cover headline, *Atlantic Monthly,* April 1993.

Chapter 10

1. Peter J. Kreeft, *Back to Virtue* (San Francisco: Ignatius Press, 1990), 180.

2. Paraphrase from Aubrey P. Andelin, *Man of Steel and Velvet* (Santa Barbara, Calif.: Pacific Press, 1972).

Chapter 11

1. Evan S. Connell, from *Mrs. Bridges and Mr. Bridges* (Viking, 1959).

2. *Time* magazine, Fall 1992 special edition, "Beyond the Year 2000: What to Expect in the New Millennium."

Chapter 12

1. Willard Harley, *His Needs, Her Needs* (Grand Rapids, Mich.: Fleming H. Revell, a division of Baker Book House Company), 118.

2. Mariam Arond and Samuel Pauker, M.D., *The First Year of Marriage* (New York: Warner Books, Inc., 1987), 162-3.

Chapter 13

1. William Shakespeare, *The Taming of the Shrew,* act II, scene 1.

2. Walter Wangerin Jr., *As for Me and My House* (Nashville, Tenn.: Thomas Nelson, Inc., 1987), 31.

Chapter 14

1. Bob Phillips, *A Humorous Look at Love and Marriage* (Eugene, Oreg.: Harvest House, 1981), 54-57.

2. "A Defense of Rash Vows," *Brave New Family, G. K. Chesterton on Men and Women, Children, Sex, Divorce, Marriage and the Family* (Ignatius Press, 1990), 52.